COPYRIGHT © 2014 BY NEFER KHEPRI
Library of Congress Control Number: 2014949919

All rights reserved. No part of this work may be reproduced or used in any form or by any means—graphic, electronic, or mechanical, including photocopying or information storage and retrieval systems—without written permission from the publisher. The scanning, uploading and distribution of this book or any part thereof via the Internet or via any other means without the permission of the publisher is illegal and punishable by law. Please purchase only authorized editions and do not participate in or encourage the electronic piracy of copyrighted materials. "Schiffer," "Schiffer Publishing, Ltd. and Design," and the "Design of pen and inkwell" are registered trademarks of Schiffer Publishing, Ltd.

Designed by Danielle D. Farmer
Type set in Nouveau/Arial

ISBN: 978-0-7643-4776-4
Printed in China

Schiffer Books are available at special discounts for bulk purchases for sales promotions or premiums. Special editions, including personalized covers, corporate imprints, and excerpts can be created in large quantities for special needs. For more information contact the publisher:

Published by Schiffer Publishing, Ltd.
4880 Lower Valley Road
Atglen, PA 19310
Phone: (610) 593-1777; Fax: (610) 593-2002
E-mail: Info@schifferbooks.com

For the largest selection of fine reference books on this and related subjects, please visit our website at
www.schifferbooks.com.

We are always looking for people to write books on new and related subjects. If you have an idea for a book, please contact us at proposals@schifferbooks.com.
This book may be purchased from the publisher.
Please try your bookstore first.
You may write for a free catalog.

Box image: Seamless Egyptian pattern © Gregor909. Image from www.BigStockPhoto.com.

DISCLAIMER

I always urge my clients to never use divination in place of consulting a professional if such consultation is warranted, such as: a doctor, lawyer, therapist, or psychiatrist.

Divination, whether it is with Lenormand cards, Tarot cards, or any other method, is not meant to replace professional guidance from those well trained in their respective fields.

The author acknowledges no responsibility whatsoever regarding the use of *The Egyptian Lenormand* or any decisions or actions taken as a result of a reading with this deck.

Your future is your own to make of it what you will. It is my hope your steps are always divinely guided in the direction of your highest good and the highest good of all concerned.

CONTENTS

DEDICATION 4

ACKNOWLEDGMENTS 6

PREFACE 7

INTRODUCTION 8

INTERPRETATIONS OF THE CARDS ___ 10

   1 RIDER 10
   2 CLOVER 12
   3 SHIP 13
   4 HOUSE 14
   5 TREE 15
   6 CLOUDS 16
   7 SNAKE 18
   8 SARCOPHAGUS 20
   9 FLOWERS 22
  10 SICKLE 24
  11 CROOK & FLAIL 26
  12 BIRDS 28
  13 CHILD 30
  14 DESERT FOX 31
  15 SACRED COW 33
  16 STARS 35
  17 IBIS 37
  18 THE DOG 39
  19 OBELISK 40
  20 GARDEN 42
  21 MOUNTAIN 43
  22 CROSSROADS 45
  23 MICE 46
  24 HEART 48
  25 RING 50
  26 SCROLL 52
  27 LETTER 54
  28 GOD AND PHARAOH 55
  29 GODDESS AND PRIESTESS 57
  30 WATER LILY 59
  31 SUN 61
  32 MOON 63
  33 KEY 64
  34 FISH 65
  35 ANCHOR 67
  36 DJED PILLAR 69
  37 CAT 71

HOW TO READ LENORMAND
CARDS 79

ACTIVATION OF THE DECK FOR
HEALING AND MAGIC 115

HEALTH AND HEALING 124

THE POWER OF MAGIC FOR
MANIFESTATION 148

CONCLUSION 172

REFERENCES CITED AND
RESOURCES 173

DEDICATION

For my mother, Valentina Olga Gutierrez, who passed away on January 20, 2008, from a ten-month-long illness. She was 82. She was born to two employees of Ringling Brothers Circus in 1925 (back when that circus was the king and before they partnered with P. T. Barnum). My grandpa was a tightrope walker and my grandma was a trapeze artist. Mom was born on Valentines' Day, so they named her Valentina.

Mom was born with a moderate case of spina bifida (part of the spine is exposed, fluid is lost, and it leads to all sorts of very serious problems that are lifelong). She lived through the Great Depression, was homeless with my grandpa for three years, and by the time she was 20 had undergone five major surgeries on her spine. She was in a house fire when recuperating from the last surgery. The entire house was made of wood and she was in a bedroom on the second floor. Everyone got out except my mother. So her cousin, my second-cousin Ruben Martinez, ran back into the house and carried Mom down two flights of wooden stairs that were already catching fire—the flames were right behind them. He was only 14 at the time and Mom was 20. He saved Mom's life. So in a way, this deck is for Ruben, too.

Mom was told she would never be able to hold down a job, she would certainly never drive (considering she couldn't use her feet to work the gas and brake pedals of a car), she would certainly never ever have children due to her condition, and she would not live to see 30.

Mom called mechanics all over Waukegan, Illinois, our home town, then Zion, and further into Chicago and Milwaukee until she found a man who thought he could design her hand controls to use in a car. This was in 1944 and the mechanic succeeded. Mom learned how to drive. Then she went out and got herself a job at a screw factory to help with the war effort and made the local paper for that accomplishment. She became a strong advocate on behalf of getting physically and mentally challenged people out into the workforce.

Then she defied the doctors and got pregnant. They all told her to abort me because the birthing process would ruin her spinal surgery and/or kill her and me. Mom ignored them and had me via c-section.

My mom had lived a hard life and it toughened her. She never let on until her death bed that, due to the spina bifida, she had been in constant pain her entire life. No one ever knew, not even my father, because Mom was not the type of person to complain.

After she passed away, I was going through boxes of her papers and in one I found an accordion-fold file in which she had kept some of my artwork, some dating back to when I was only 2. In that accordion-fold file there was a note dated for my 20th birthday.

Here is what it says:

My Dearest Daughter,

You are the greatest blessing God ever gave to me. When I think of all the hardship I have endured in my life all of it becomes nothing when I think of the wonderful woman you are becoming. All of it was worth it and I would do it all again at ten times worse just for the chance to see your sparkling eyes. I want you to know you can do anything you set your mind to, and I mean ANYTHING. Here is your art dating back to when you were a baby. You always loved it so much. It is my wish for you that you return to your art one day. I know one day everyone will see your art in print. I am, and always will be, so very proud of you.

All My Love,
Mom

A week before she died we all knew the end was near as Mom was then under hospice care. She told me she had a vision of me with a lot of very brightly colored cards of Egyptian items and in the color palette of ancient Egypt. I truly believe what she saw was this deck. Mom had her vision 2½ years before I even contemplated creating a Lenormand deck.

Mom, thank you for all you have ever done for me, all the sacrifices you and Dad made to send me to college, and for your love and support. I literally do owe you my life.

THIS DECK IS FOR YOU.

ACKNOWLEDGMENTS

I thank my family, my husband, Stuart, and our daughter, Ariel. There were many nights I was too tired from filling orders for my business and working on the images for this deck to cook. They never complained. They also further supported me by doing the dishes and the laundry. They truly are the lights of my life.

I also wish to thank my late parents, Roberto and Valentina Gutierrez. I was blessed to be raised by two open-minded people who thought nothing of discussing such things as ghosts and psychic experiences they had or the experiences of others. Our dinner conversations were always so interesting and I learned at an early age that the world of spirit is very real and within easy reach. They valued education above all else, instilled that love in me, and sacrificed tremendously to send me to my first choice university, Northwestern in Evanston, Illinois.

I thank Caitlín Matthews and Lisa Hunt for kindly endorsing my deck after working with an earlier self-published edition.

I further thank friends and colleagues on Facebook who not only lent their moral support throughout the creation process of this deck and the writing of the book, but also commented on earlier drafts of the cards: DenElder, Ruth Ibbotson, Salisha Noor-Birjou, and the members of my 2013 Lenormand online class.

I extend appreciation and gratitude to my editor, Dinah Roseberry, for her guidance and support during the process. I also wish to thank Pete Schiffer, whose constructive criticism of my artwork helped me to reach deeper within myself when I revised some of the cards. I additionally thank the staff at Schiffer Publishing.

Finally, I offer my sincerest appreciation to the Aspects of Deity known to us today as Isis, Osiris, Hathor, Ra, Sekhmet, Horus, Bastet, Anubis, Ma'at, Thoth, Khumn, Khepera, and Amun-Ra for granting me the tremendous blessing of using me as their channel to share these images and this information with the public. Without them this project would never have come into being.

PREFACE

I began working on what was to become *The Egyptian Lenormand* in September 2012. At the time, I didn't realize that what I was doing was creating a Lenormand deck. I am a practicing Wiccan and I work with several of the Egyptian deities. They began to send me images including color schemes. Once I received four images, I realized what the gods and I were developing together was to be a Lenormand deck.

Every image is channeled. I was told via clairaudience, or sometimes in visions, what to draw. For some cards, I was shown the card fully developed and then all I had to do was create it from memory. In other cases, the gods merely told me what they wished to be depicted on the card. For example, when the gods had me create The Sun card, they told me they wished for an image of Khepera to be depicted pushing the sun across the sky. So that's what I drew, and they then provided me with a psychic vision of the completed image. The only exception to this was The Child card. That is the only card in the entire deck that is not channeled from the gods. I had been trying for days to draw a portrait of a child, but was quickly discovering I am unable to draw children. My daughter, Ariel, suggested that I research ancient Egyptian children's toys online and draw several of those instead of an actual child. So, I am thankful to my daughter for her wise counsel on what to do about the troublesome Child card. It is now one of my personal favorites.

All images were hand drawn with drafting pencil on Strathmore Bristol Smooth card stock. I used a combination of Faber-Castel Polychromos pencils, Faber-Castel watercolor pencils, Prismacolor pencils, and Caran D'Ache water soluable crayons for the backgrounds. I went over the lines with Copic black ink markers in various nib sizes.

I completed the deck late on Valentine's Day, February 14, 2013, in time for it to be completed as I had originally hoped, on what would have been my mother's 87th birthday.

INTRODUCTION

Lenormand is a system of divination using a deck of 36 cards that became popular in France and Germany during the time of Napoleon. The Lenormand was developed by Johann Kaspar of Germany, in 1798, and was meant initially to be used as a game originally called, "The Game of Hope" (Riding, 2013). The name of the system of divination we use today is derived from a woman who gained great renown as a Lenormand reader, the famous French fortune-teller Marie Anne Adelaide Lenormand. Although she has never been documented using an actual Lenormand deck, her name was given to this system of divination as a way to popularize it through connection to her and her reputation as a reader of renown.

HOW IS LENORMAND DIFFERENT FROM TAROT?

Basically, a Lenormand reading will tell you like it is—clear, concise, and full of details about what you can expect. A Tarot reading, on the other hand, offers you advice and general guidance, especially of a spiritual nature.

The Tarot consists of 78 cards: 22 Major Arcana and 56 Minor Arcana (upon which our modern playing cards are based upon). The Tarot deals with universal archetypical forces at work in our lives (Major Arcana cards) that affect our mundane lives in various ways (Minor Arcana).

The Lenormand, on the other hand, has only 36 cards in total. These cards are associated with particular playing cards of the modern playing card deck, and many Lenormand decks will include a small picture insert of their corresponding playing card. Cards are named with such titles as: The Rider, Clover, Ship, Bouquet, Ring, and Moon. The images are very simple. For instance, The Ring is a picture of a ring, The Ship is a picture of a ship, and so on.

Card combinations in any Lenormand reading are of paramount importance. Cards will take on different meanings when paired with other cards. In any Lenormand reading that I do, I offer the traditional interpretation of the card, then I look closely at all nearby cards and discuss the meanings of all the various card combinations. This is how the Lenormand provides you with the full picture of any type of situation or question.

WHAT SORT OF QUESTIONS CAN I ASK FOR A LENORMAND READING?

I have come to find out through my own use that the Lenormand can address any type of question. My only restriction is a personal one. I do not read on matters of health; however, due to The Tree card that represents health (also stability and longevity) in the Lenormand system, Health will be generally discussed for any reading in which The Tree appears, but I remind everyone never use readings or candle work in place of consulting a doctor or other health care professional.

I have had people ask questions about their relationships (romantic and otherwise), their children and other family members, their pets, spiritual growth, past lives, dreams, careers/jobs, and so on. I have, so far, not run across any topic that the Lenormand cannot handle in a reading.

When coming to the Lenormand with a question, just as with Tarot, the same rule holds: the more specific your question is the more direct and specific your reading will be.

HOW LONG DOES IT TAKE TO DO A LENORMAND READING?

That depends on the type of spread you choose to use for your reading. A spread is the configuration in which cards are placed on a table for a reading. The time required will vary based on the time you wish to spend on your reading.

In this guide, I will discuss the manner in which Lenormand cards are read and provide examples of actual readings using the 3- and 5-card spreads commonly used in Lenormand and cartomancy in general, and a more involved 10-card reading called The Pyramid of Isis that I created specifically for use with *The Egyptian Lenormand*.

This deck goes beyond divination and can also be used in order to channel healing energy for yourself and others.

Finally, information is also shared as to how *The Egyptian Lenormand* can also be put to magical use.

INTERPRETATIONS OF THE CARDS

CARD 1 | RIDER

The card interpretations offered here follow traditional Lenormand card meanings that are very similar from source to source. I also include a brief description of the Egyptian symbol's usage and or meaning in ancient Egypt that can add a deeper layer of meaning to the card, if you so desire. For those of you who practice the art of cartomancy, each card's playing card association is noted in the upper right-hand corner in shorthand, such as Jack of Diamonds is noted as JD, the Ace of Hearts is noted as AH, and so on. Diamonds are "D", Clubs are "C", Spades are "S", and Hearts are "H".

I always like to point out to clients that just because a reading says something will happen, does not make it so. Readings work within the laws of probability. The outcome of a reading is based upon current behaviors, attitudes, and beliefs. Change any of those and you can change the outcome. This is a good thing to keep in mind if you receive a reading for which you do not like the outcome. Change your present and you therefore change your future.

Keywords: Message bearer, young man, travel over short distances, news

Playing Card Association: 9 of Hearts (9H)

The Rider usually represents a person, like the mailman, the UPS delivery man, etc. This person brings something to you. It can be a message or an item. Sometimes he brings news by word of mouth. This card can even appear to represent a friend who brings you a juicy piece of gossip.

The card that follows the Rider will tell you what the Rider is bringing to you. Paired with Flowers, the Rider is bringing you a gift. Paired with the Djed Pillar, the Rider is bringing you something (news, message, or an item) that may cause you some grief. Paired with the Obelisk, the Rider is bringing news that is dealing with an authority figure or institution of some kind, etc.

Whenever you receive the Rider in a reading, always look to the next card to see what he brings you. If he is the last card of a reading and you are not doing a Grand Tableau spread, by all means feel free to draw an additional card at random from the remaining cards to discover what is making its way to you.

Many Lenormand readers associate the Rider card with the knees, legs, and/or ankles, so if you're reading about health, the presence of the Rider card can indicate something is going on with that part of the body. (Boroveshengra 2014, Steinbach 2007:8)

RIDER:
ANCIENT EGYPTIAN MEANING

This is much the same as the traditional Lenormand meaning shared above. Back in ancient Egypt, there were two main methods of transportation: the horse and the camel. The horse was used mainly by the nobility, while the commoners who were financially better off than others might afford horses, but most would have used camels, since horses were very expensive to maintain.

For my version of the Rider card, I chose to depict a man on a camel on an outcrop overlooking the Giza Plateau. You can see the Great Pyramid of Kheops in the background. For the Rider, I chose a modern-day Bedouin man as my model. Very little has changed for the Bedouins over the succeeding millennia and he would have looked very much the same back in ancient Egyptian times as well.

The camel was the ideal animal for use in desert transportation. The wide pads on its feet allowed the animal to walk steadily on shifting sands, even while carrying a heavy load. They were most often used as pack animals and the camel's keeper would walk alongside the animal. Merchants would carry their goods on a very long caravan of camels across the desert to and from Egypt carrying their exotic wares.

The camel stores water in its hump on its back; therefore, it has its own reservoir of energy in terms of keeping itself hydrated in the intense desert heat. The camel on the Rider card indicates you have your own wealth of a reservoir, but you may need to dig down deep within yourself to find the energy or resources you need to carry out the task at hand.

INTERPRETATIONS OF THE CARDS

CARD 2 | CLOVER

Keywords: Luck, short-lived opportunities, small change of fortune, happiness

Playing Card Association: 6 of Diamonds (6D)

The Clover represents a turn of luck that may be fleeting. It's best to keep your eyes open for new opportunities when Clover lands in your reading. They may be short-lived, so you may be required to make a quick decision and act fast in order to take full advantage of the opportunities indicated. The Clover can also represent a small change of fortune like a stroke of good luck, but again, it won't last long, so be sure when it occurs to take full advantage of the good vibrations while they last.

When read in pairs, the card following The Clover can tell you what sort of luck is coming your way. For example, Clover followed by Fish or Sacred Cow may indicate a small and unexpected windfall. Perhaps you'll find some money on the ground or receive a small bonus incentive at work. Clover + Ring can indicate a fortuitous partnership that will bring luck to both people involved.

CLOVER:

ANCIENT EGYPTIAN MEANING

There is nothing documented that I was able to find as to how ancient Egyptians viewed Clover or what they may have thought about it. There is actually a type of clover called Egyptian Clover and that is what I depicted on this card. According to Oushy (2008), Egyptian Clover was an important crop during the winter in Egypt. It was cultivated and used as fertilizer for the soil and is known to this day for its ability to add nitrogen content to it. It is still cultivated for this purpose. The ancient Egyptians cultivated Egyptian Clover for use as a soil fertilizer and during the winter months, it was used as feed for animals. It also had medicinal uses.

CARD 3 | SHIP

Keywords: travel, journey, trip, movement

Playing Card Association: 10 of Spades (10S)

Ships, like the one depicted on this card, and barges, were important modes of transportation in ancient Egypt. The Nile River was like a modern-day highway, cluttered with ships and boats of all sizes. Ship represents travel and usually indicates travel over water. These days, the actual mode of transportation may not be an actual ship, but a plane. Ship can also indicate a journey or movement forward or back in a situation, depending on surrounding cards.

Water was of crucial importance to the ancient Egyptians being a desert people. They viewed water as life-sustaining. Ship can also indicate the importance of water in your life for your health and cleanliness, and it can also represent the subconscious.

SHIP:
ANCIENT EGYPTIAN MEANING

Ships were used to travel up and down the River Nile moving people, animals, and goods. Special barges with enclosed rooms, like the one depicted on this card, were used to house the nobility during their travels. Even statues of gods had their own barges and, when they were taken to other towns for special festivals, they had their own ship and personal attendants for the journey.

INTERPRETATIONS OF THE CARDS

CARD 4 | HOUSE

Keywords: Home, Domesticity, Stability, Peace, Harmony, Safety, Security, Family

Playing Card Association: King of Hearts (KH)

The House card represents the physical house and the home environment. The House card can indicate events that occur within the home, such as family gatherings, meals, celebrations, and so on. The home is viewed as the source of safety and security. A happy home is a stable home. The House card indicates feelings of peacefulness and harmony.

The card that follows House in a reading will tell you what is going on in the home. For example, House + Dog may very well indicate the family pet or discussions about getting a dog. House + Rider may indicate a visitor or someone coming to your home bearing important news.

HOUSE:
ANCIENT EGYPTIAN MEANING

Low-lying tables were used by the ancient Egyptian commoners who would then sit on blankets and pillows around the table for the family meal. Beds could be located along the walls in the form of a long shelf or as pallets on the floor in separate rooms for those members of society who were somewhat wealthy and could afford the luxury of extra rooms serving as bedrooms.

The cat was domesticated in ancient Egypt. Sacred to the goddess Bastet, as well as to many other gods and goddesses, the cat was the most popular pet in ancient Egypt. Many homes had at least one household kitty in residence and here you can see him napping under the table.

CARD 5 | TREE

Keywords: Longevity, Stability, Health, Vitality, Ancestry, Foundation, Grounding, Rebirth

Playing Card Association: 7 of Hearts (7H)

When the Tree appears in a reading it will often represent something that is strong and stable. To the right of the Heart, this card combination would indicate strong cardiovascular health or a stable relationship. To the right of Fish, the combination indicates a stable source of income or prosperity that will be long lived. The Tree is strong, vital, green and healthy; therefore, it is also associated with physical health. If you use *The Egyptian Lenormand* to ask questions about health matters, Tree would represent your health and the card that follows Tree in the reading would further describe the state of health of the individual. For example, in a health reading Tree + Clover would be a small improvement in health or the start of the healing process. Tree + Sun would indicate a major healing or huge improvement in one's health, as also would Tree + Flowers.

Tree can also appear pertaining to your family, extended family, and even your ancestors. In some cases, it can be a card of Karma as well, especially if falling next to the Djed Pillar card. Tree will indicate strong family ties unless it is landing near negative cards, such as Snake and Desert Fox, which can then represent a family member who may be a bit of a problem.

The roots of trees reach far into the ground; therefore, the Tree card is also symbolic of grounding one's energy into the earth. The presence of Tree in a reading may indicate that you either need to ground your energy more effectively or that you already have firm roots where your energy is concerned. Tree also can represent a firm foundation of whatever type of card precedes it. For example, Dog + Tree would indicate a firm foundation in a friendship. Let's say you're concerned about the

15

INTERPRETATIONS OF THE CARDS

stability of the foundation of your house and are worried there could be structural problems. House + Tree would indicate a firm house foundation and therefore no real need to worry or consult a contractor.

TREE:

ANCIENT EGYPTIAN MEANING

I drew this image of a date palm tree (common throughout northern Africa) based loosely upon a stylized tomb painting of a date palm. I chose the date palm tree as opposed to a regular palm tree because dates are very healthy for you and I wanted to convey the meaning of "health" and "vitality" with this image.

The color green to the ancient Egyptians denoted resurrection (the resurrected god Osiris is depicted as God of Agriculture with a green face). Therefore, in *The Egyptian Lenormand* the Tree card can also signify rebirth.

CARD 6 | CLOUDS

Keywords: Confusion, Miscommunication, Misunderstanding, Mental Issues, Complications

Playing Card Association: King of Clubs (KC)

The Clouds in a reading may indicate that all is not as it seems. Clouds can represent seeing things through a fog or perhaps missing the finer details pertaining to the situation under question. Therefore, Clouds can be warning you to pay closer attention. You may need a second opinion regarding the matter under question or have it better explained to you.

Clouds can indicate confusion about something or someone. They warn that you may be second-guessing yourself, when you should rely upon your intuition. You may not be sure what to think.

Clouds can also point to miscommunication and misunderstandings between individuals that leads to feelings of confusion. This card may indicate that a discussion has turned sour. The Clouds card denote a lack of clarity. The situation could be in flux, a process of change or evolution and you may not be aware of everything that's going on behind the scenes.

The situation you are asking about is either complicated in and of itself or it may be plagued by complications. The Clouds in health matters represent mental issues, especially such illnesses as Parkinson's Disease in which dementia may be involved. However, traditionally, Clouds regarding the physical body represent the respiratory system. (Boroveshengra 2014, Steinbach 2007:28)

The Clouds card is one of the very few in the Lenormand system for which directionality is very important. Most decks have the Clouds card show sunny clouds on one side, darker grayer clouds on the other. For my image I chose to place the sunny side on the left-hand side of the card and the grayer clouds on the right. When Clouds appears in a reading, note which cards land on the sunny side of the card and which cards land on the cloudy or darker side of the card. The card to the right will be what the Clouds card is affecting. For example, if you receive the combination of Clouds + Letter you know you can look forward to receiving some confusing or unclear communication via the written word, whether that's an actual physical letter, email, fax, or text.

CLOUDS:
ANCIENT EGYPTIAN MEANING

Rain in ancient Egypt, as today, was quite infrequent, with an average rainfall of 2–5 mm each winter. The River Nile floods annually, however, not from rain, but from the melting of the ice caps of the mountains of Sinai. Consequently, it was the Nile and not rainfall that was considered the source of agricultural fertility. Homes of the general population were constructed from unbaked mud bricks. Therefore, any significant amount of rainfall could prove to be disastrous using such construction methods.

INTERPRETATIONS OF THE CARDS

CARD 7 | SNAKE

Keywords: Treachery, Betrayal, Deceit, Warning, Danger, Circuitous

Playing Card Association: Queen of Clubs (QC)

Traditionally in Lenormand, the Snake is viewed as an older woman. Depending on surrounding cards, she may or may not be deceitful and untrustworthy. Therefore, the context in which this card appears is very important. Be sure to closely examine surrounding cards.

The Snake card can appear in a reading to represent a warning. It may be identifying the card before it as a source of danger. For example, let's say you're contemplating meeting a man you have gotten to know online. He appears in your reading as the Pharaoh card followed immediately by Snake. This card combination is telling you he is untrustworthy and may even be dangerous. Another type of warning can be regarding a journey you are planning. Ship appears as representing the trip and is followed by Snake, which can mean you will encounter either a dangerous situation or person on the trip, so you need to take precautions.

The Snake can indicate manipulation, lies, and betrayal. Once again, the context in which the card appears is very important. For example, you may be asking about some new friends and the Dog card appears, but it is followed by the Snake. This may indicate that this group of friends is not for your highest good and one or more of them may intend to betray you at some point.

Snake, due to the manner in which it slithers across the ground, represents taking the long way around to going somewhere or doing something. You have a direct route in mind, but if Snake appears, you can expect some unexpected detours.

At its worst, in *The Egyptian Lenormand,* the Snake card can represent an evil energy or entity. This would depend upon the question being asked and the context in which the Snake card appears.

SNAKE:
ANCIENT EGYPTIAN MEANING

The Snake card here is based on a depiction of Apep, a snake deity portrayed in the ancient *Egyptian Book of the Dead*, or *The Book of Coming Forth By Day*, as it was known in ancient times. Apep is a creature of the Duat and he roams the underworld in search of lost souls to consume. As the sun sinks below the horizon to start its nightly journey through the Duat (Egyptian underworld), Apep attempts to attack and eat the sun. The sun god Ra fights off Apep every night, sometimes aided by other gods, such as Bastet and Thoth. Ra is always victorious and the sun rises once again each day.

Apep was considered by the ancient Egyptians to be an incarnation of evil. Therefore, the ground across which the Snake slithers on this card is red, for the color red was associated with evil, chaos, and disease by the ancient Egyptians. It was also associated with the desert and all animals that dwelled within the desert, such as snakes, scorpions, jackels, hyenas, and the desert fox.

INTERPRETATIONS OF THE CARDS

CARD 8 | SARCOPHAGUS

Keywords: Illness, Depression, Endings, the Dead

Playing Card Association: 9 of Diamonds (9D)

Traditionally in Lenormand, card number 8 is named The Coffin. However, in keeping with the cultural significance of symbols from ancient Egypt for *The Egyptian Lenormand*, I chose to depict a sarcophagus.

The Sarcophagus card in a reading can indicate a situation or person who is experiencing some type of ending in their life. It can point to the conclusion of a cycle and perhaps the beginning of another. The Sarcophagus can represent the end of something. For instance, Ring + Sarcophagus would suggest the end of a partnership or marriage; Dog + Sarcophagus, the end of a friendship; Ship + Sarcophagus, the end of a journey.

The Coffin card in other Lenormand decks can represent depression or grief over someone's passing. The Sarcophagus here has the same meaning. However, the ancient Egyptians strongly believed in an afterlife, so although a person may be in

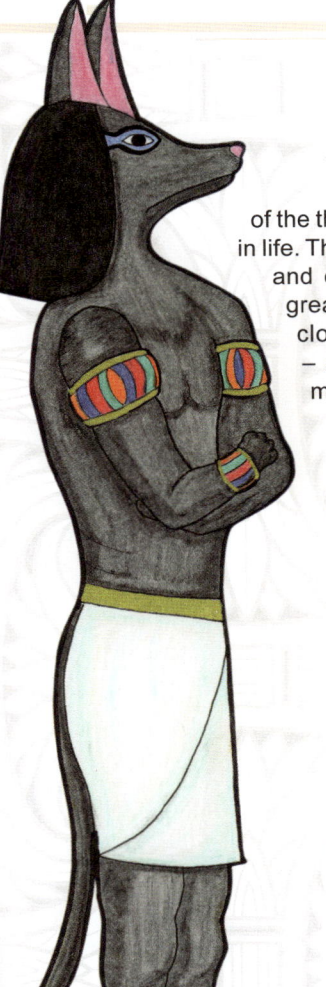

deep mourning over the loss of a loved one, the Sarcophagus is an important reminder that the Soul is eternal. The Soul is pure energy that can never be destroyed. Through death, the Soul takes on another form, thus undergoes a transformation. The Sarcophagus is a reminder that we will be reunited with our departed loved ones, according to your own personal beliefs.

Sometimes the Sarcophagus card can represent the Dead, or spirits. However, this would depend on the question you are asking and the context in which the card appears. If you are, for example, asking if your house is haunted and Sarcophagus shows up in a prominent position in the spread, then chances are good your suspicions are correct.

Sarcophagus:
ANCIENT EGYPTIAN MEANING

The Egyptians believed in eternal life and that those who successfully passed the tests and tribulations that their soul was put through in the Duat (underworld) would ascend to the heavens to become one of the stars. They believed that, once among the stars, the body would resurrect and would, therefore, have need of the things that the person had used in life. The tombs of pharaohs, queens, and other nobility were filled with great finery, food, wine, furniture, clothing, make-up, and dishes – anything and everything they may need in the next life.

INTERPRETATIONS OF THE CARDS

CARD 9 | FLOWERS

Keywords: Gift, Nice Surprise, Happiness, Improvements, Healing, Invitation

Playing Card Association: Queen of Spades (QS)

Flowers bring up thoughts of happiness, spring time, birds chirping, and the fallow earth coming back to vibrant life after a long winter. The Flowers card can denote timing. What you are asking about may most likely occur in the spring season. When Flowers appears in a reading, it indicates a general improvement regarding the situation you are inquiring about. Things are looking up!

Flowers also can represent a gift coming your way that may or may not be expected. People give flowers when they are courting and for special occasions. This is how the Flowers card came to be associated with gift-giving. An example of Flowers meaning a gift: I did a three-card draw one time, just for a general reading for the day. I received Rider + Flowers + House. Rider brings things to you: messages, parcels, information, etc. Flowers I took to mean a gift, so Rider + Flowers meant I was to receive a gift that day. House meant it was coming to my house. So in this case, since it wasn't a special day, I figured the UPS man was bringing me a delivery I hadn't ordered, so I wasn't expecting anything. I was amazed when not two hours later, the bell rang. It was the UPS man and he had this huge box. I was even more amazed when I opened the box. It contained a singing crystal bowl sent to me as a "just because I love you gift" from a very dear friend of mine! I was so touched, I cried. So, here is an excellent example of how Lenormand can be incredibly literal and accurate.

FLOWERS:
ANCIENT EGYPTIAN MEANING

The Flowers card is a depiction of papyrus flowers portrayed in the style of ancient Egypt. Palace and tomb walls were frequently decorated with depictions of papyrus flowers and carvings of them graced the tops of columns used in architecture. The papyrus plant was very important in ancient Egypt. From the plant fibers, the ancient Egyptians invented paper. This allowed for writing to flourish and provided a more efficient means of record-keeping than carving on clay tablets as their contemporaries, the Sumerians, were doing at the time.

According to Seid (2004), the earliest use of papyrus dates back to approximately 2,600 B.C. Scribes would write on a single side of the papyrus that would then either be folded, or more usually rolled up. When multiple pages were needed, the papyrus sheets would be adhered together in a codex style, which was the precursor to the form of the book as we know it today. In fact, our word for "paper" derives from the word, "papyrus."

For the ancient Egyptians, the papyrus was viewed as symbolic of prosperity, for only the wealthy and nobility could afford to possess it. The Egyptians kept the method of papyrus paper production a closely guarded secret for centuries. It was a major export of Egypt and they also used papyrus in the production of baskets, sandals, boats, fuel, rope, and medicine (unknown author, 2010). Since the papyrus plant was also used for medicinal purposes, I chose it as my symbol for the Flowers card because, in traditional Lenormand, Flowers can also indicate healing; plus, the flowers of the plant were held sacred by ancient Egyptians.

INTERPRETATIONS OF THE CARDS

CARD 10 | SICKLE

Keywords: Cutting or Cuts/Abrasions, Separation, Dividing, Danger, Accidents, Harvest

Playing Card Association: Jack of Diamonds (JD)

 Sickle (otherwise known as Scythe in other Lenormand decks), is one of the very few cards in the Lenormand system for which directionality is very important. Whenever Sickle appears in a reading, always pay close attention to the direction in which the blade points. I designed this card so the blade points to the right. What this means is whatever card lands to the right of Sickle will identify what is to be cut, separated, divided, harmed, or what may be in some type of danger. As with the Clouds card, direction for the Sickle is very important and can greatly alter the interpretation of your reading.

 The Sickle is a tool of ancient agriculture used by civilizations all around the world. The Sickle was used to cut down the crops in order to harvest them. Thus, the Sickle card is strongly associated with cutting, separating, and even cuts and abrasions, since many farmers probably cut themselves with their sickles. It also represents danger because, in untrained hands, it can be a very dangerous tool, while, in trained hands, it can become a dangerous weapon.

Despite its negative connotations, Sickle does have a positive side. Depending on how it appears in a reading, this card can indicate a harvest, a reaping of what you have sown. The item being harvested will appear to the left of the Sickle card, so the blade depicted on the card will be cutting away from the item. For example, let's say you're asking if you will receive a raise or promotion at work and your reading has the card combination of Fish + Sickle. Fish represents prosperity and is the money card in the Lenormand system. So, in this case based upon the question you were asking, Fish + Sickle would indicate a harvest of money, so the answer would be yes, you can look forward to a raise, promotion, or both.

SICKLE:

ANCIENT EGYPTIAN MEANING

Sickles in ancient Egypt were made from a curved piece of wood mimicking the shape of a cow's jaw into which obsidian blades were placed where the teeth would be located in a cow. It was set into a wooden handle that was then wrapped with tanned animal hide. Sickles were handheld. A very narrow groove was etched into the edge of the wooden curve into which small blades were fitted and adhered. The blades were hand carved from narrow strips of tan or brown obsidian (Stead, 1986). Obsidian is volcanic glass. It is the sharpest cutting tool known to man and was commonly used by many civilizations throughout the ancient world.

I worked in an archaeology lab at Northwestern University as an undergraduate and I can vouch for the ability of an obsidian blade to EASILY slice into a finger. The cut was so fine that I didn't even feel it or see any blood until I leaned on the table with my hand; then I discovered I was bleeding. These days, some surgeons insist on using only surgical tools made of obsidian and maintain that it makes a finer incision than conventional modern surgical tools.

INTERPRETATIONS OF THE CARDS

CARD 11 | CROOK & FLAIL

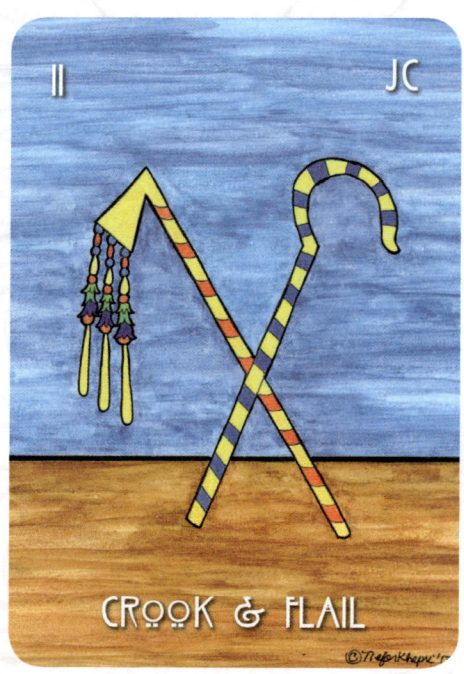

Keywords: Impassioned Arguments, Discussions, Harsh Words, Abuse, Anger, Judgment

Playing Card Association: Jack of Clubs (JC)

    The Crook & Flail is used as the image for the more traditional Lenormand "Whip," "Broom," or "Rod" card. It goes by all three names. Although ancient Egyptians also had whips, I wanted to go with a more Egyptian image that would convey the same traditional Lenormand meaning as the Whip card of other Lenormand decks. I chose the Crook & Flail due to its ancient symbolic associations.

    The Crook & Flail were carried by Pharaoh for most state occasions and especially when foreign dignitaries would visit his court. The Crook was symbolic of his care and concern for his people, while the flail represented his willingness to use whatever force necessary to keep enemies at bay and protect his vast lands and holdings. The Crook & Flail are associated with fair judgment, but also with harshness and even cruelty and abuse when it came to the enemies of the Egyptian state. In some cases, as a number of the Pharaohs were corrupt, the Crook & Flail are also symbolic of the abuse of power.

In a reading, the Crook & Flail will usually appear to indicate either the exchanging of harsh words, an argument, or disagreement. The card to the right will tell you the topic or reason behind the issue.

The Flail was used by many ancient Egyptians as a tool of everyday life. It consisted of a short wooden poll to which strands of beads were attached. Ancient Egypt suffered from very serious fly infestations, and the people were forced to use the Flail in order to flick flies away from them and their food. Over time, the Flail came to be associated with flicking away small annoyances and was a symbol used by Pharaoh to instill his authority into his words when issuing royal decrees.

CROOK & FLAIL:
ANCIENT EGYPTIAN MEANING

The ancient use of the Crook, the rounded hook, involved the herding of animals. Shepherds used the Crook to gather up wayward animals and lambs that had strayed too far from the flock. Later on in ancient Egyptian history, the Crook therefore became a symbol of keeping the masses in line—and of exerting power over them. Thus, the Crook came to be associated with firmness and, when needed, aggression or even violence—a far cry from its original use.

INTERPRETATIONS OF THE CARDS

CARD 12 | BIRDS

Keywords: Verbal Communication, Gossip, Two of Something, Negotiation, Minor Stress

Playing Card Association: 7 of Diamonds (7D)

The Birds card (in some Lenormand decks this is called Owls and will show a pair of them) in a reading usually represents verbal exchanges occurring; for instance, conversations, phone calls, and such. It represents an exchange of information and ideas between two people or sometimes more. The Birds can also indicate gossip among friends and it can point to someone talking about you behind your back, depending on its placement in your reading.

The Birds card is associated with the number two and usually only two birds are depicted on this card to hold to that tradition, which I have also shown here. The number two can indicate a couple, and if so, they will usually be older. The number two can also represent something will happen "in two," as in two days, weeks, or months.

The Birds card represents civil discussions (unlike the Crook & Flail card that represents arguments), coming to an agreement about something that is hopefully mutually beneficial to all concerned parties, and sometimes it can indicate the tiny annoyances of everyday life. The card that follows Birds will tell you what the discussion will encompass. For instance, if you're asking about work and you receive Birds + Fish, Fish represents money and finances, so this tells you a discussion will occur at work that will focus upon money. This may be you asking for a raise or it could be a discussion with the financial team about the company's overall financial outlook for the quarter. Surrounding cards will offer you more details or you can always draw an additional card or two as well.

BIRDS:

ANCIENT EGYPTIAN MEANING

For the Birds, I chose to depict the *Ba*, the spiritual double of the living person, which is the human-headed bird on the right-hand side, with the god Horus the Younger, which is the falcon on the left-hand side of the card. Horus, the son of Isis and Osiris, is a solar deity so He is often depicted with a sun disk on the top of his head. The Ba depicted here belongs to a pharaoh, hence it wears a simplified version of the white crown of Upper Egypt, called the Hedjet.

Horus and the Ba of the pharaoh are having a discussion in the Duat, the Egyptian underworld. The Duat was believed to be in the sky, yet also have its own sky itself, so I chose to depict the nighttime sky as the ground and a darker daytime sky above the images. Horus and the Ba stand on an altar decorated with ankhs, the symbol of life and breath that is situated between two pillars. Pillars are symbolic of authority—here, the authority of Horus. The altar represents the action occurring in a holy or sacred location. Ancient Egyptians believed their pharaohs were the physical incarnation of Osiris or Horus. Here, the Ba of Pharaoh is giving an accounting of his deeds to Horus. A very important discussion, indeed!

INTERPRETATIONS OF THE CARDS

CARD 13 | CHILD

Keywords: Innocence, Fresh Start, Newness, Small, Playfulness, Joy

Playing Card Association: Jack of Spades (JS)

For most Lenormand decks, the artist chooses to depict The Child card with the drawing of an actual child. I chose ancient Egyptian toys instead. I see The Child card as representing joy and playfulness most commonly in readings I do for myself, so in keeping with that theme I chose toys as the image.

When The Child appears in a reading, it can represent an actual physical child. The Child card can be either male or female and nearby cards will provide additional details about this individual.

Children are innocent so The Child card can represent innocence in a reading or seeing the world, perhaps, through rose-colored glasses. It can indicate idealism or looking at something from a new or fresh perspective. The Child card represents "newness" in general. This can be a fresh start or starting something new, like a project. The Child can even come up in a reading to represent something small in size.

CHILD:

ANCIENT EGYPTIAN MEANING

I researched ancient Egyptian children's toys. It was very common for fathers to carve either wooden tops (upper right side of the card) or push-or-pull toys (the horse and bird), and then to paint them in bright colors. Tops and push/pull toys were very popular with ancient Egyptian children. Fathers would also carve a doll from a single plank of wood for their daughters. Archaeologists refer to them as "plank dolls" due to being carved from a simple plank of wood (Austin, n. d.). They were then brightly painted and short strands of beads would be attached to the head of the doll to serve as hair. My drawing for the Child card comes from actual photographs of Egyptian toys that are now housed in various museum collections.

CARD 14 | DESERT FOX

Keywords: Lies, Trickery, Cunning, High Intelligence, Manipulation, Caution, Plots

Playing Card Association: 9 of Clubs (9C)

Many Lenormand readers view The Fox as the Work card. Others choose The Moon or The Anchor. There is no set rule as to which to choose, but do make a decision based upon how you feel about the card and its interpretation, and then stick to it, and that card will be your Work card when it appears in readings.

Desert Fox in a reading can indicate that someone is lying or attempting to trick you. A person signified by the Desert Fox card is usually very intelligent and cunning. However, they will usually put their intelligence toward nefarious ends. The Desert Fox can also point to something being incorrect. For example, if it follows Ring and you are asking about a business partnership, Desert Fox would indicate that this partnership (signified by Ring) has one or more issues and may not be for your highest good.

Desert Fox can indicate the need for caution in a situation due to something unexpected, or chaotic energy entering the situation. For example, I read for a client who was going on a business trip overseas. He was asking how his family would be without him. Part of his reading consisted of the combination of House + Desert Fox. I told him this meant caution was required in or around his home. I drew the additional card of Mountain, which can represent an enemy or major obstacles. I interpreted this to mean that while he was gone, his family might experience some type of problem with the house. I felt it could be structural. Sure enough, while he was gone, his wife called him to say they had developed a roof leak in the attic and their son discovered it when he was sent up to place something there for storage. Desert Fox, in this case, was a warning to watch out for something going wrong with his house while he was away that, if left unchecked, would have caused a great deal of chaos.

INTERPRETATIONS OF THE CARDS

When Desert Fox appears in a reading it can indicate that there is something going on that you are unaware of or partially unaware. It may indicate that a person close to you is hiding their true intentions and should not be trusted. Sometimes people wear a mask in order to pretend to be something they are not. That is why I depicted a mask on this card. Finally, the Desert Fox card can represent a manipulative, cunning individual who is constantly coming up with plots. It may indicate that an idea is a get-rich-quick scheme that will not have long lasting benefits.

DESERT FOX:
ANCIENT EGYPTIAN MEANING

The Desert Fox is a breed of fox common to northeastern Africa. It exists today in Egypt and was also present during ancient times. The ancient Egyptians viewed the desert as dangerous and as a wasteland. The desert became synonymous with danger and chaos. Animals of the desert were usually seen as representing danger: snakes, scorpions, and of course the desert fox. The desert fox lived on the fringe of human society, often sneaking into villages to pilfer food. Consequently, it was seen as a sneaky intruder.

The image on the right is of the god, Set. Set was viewed as a god of the desert; therefore, he was associated with chaos, storms, and the animals of the desert. According to Egyptian mythology, Set was manipulative and was not to be trusted. When his brother, Osiris, was made Pharaoh, Set was jealous. He killed his own brother because he wanted the throne of Egypt for himself. When he discovered that Isis was pregnant with Horus, who would be the rightful heir to the throne as the son of Osiris, Set went searching for them. He employed his minions, the animals of the desert (scorpions, snakes, hyenas, and the desert fox) to look for them. He never did succeed in murdering his nephew, and years later, when Horus grew to manhood, he defeated Set in an epic battle and regained the throne of Egypt.

The background color of this card is red. Red is Set's color and he was seen as having red hair. According to Watterson (1999:102), red was also the color that the ancient Egyptians associated with the desert, which they also saw as being dangerous, arid, and the place where the dead would roam, while the black, fertile soil along either side of the Nile was the source of agricultural abundance and fertility. Therefore, red was a negative color and black was positive. The color red had negative connotations and can also be seen as the ground on The Snake card.

CARD 15 | SACRED COW

Keywords: Prosperity, Windfall, Finances, Protection, Mother

Playing Card Association: 10 of Clubs (10C)

Card 15 is usually called The Bear. However, there were no bears in ancient Egypt and I wanted to remain true to the culture, as well as the traditional meanings of the Lenormand cards, so I chose the Sacred Cow as the image because, to the ancient Egyptians, the Sacred Cow had the same meanings as the Bear to the Europeans.

Sacred Cow is considered sacred because the animal guise of the goddess Hathor was that of a cow. Hathor is the goddess of abundance, love, and happiness. She is further seen as a goddess of prosperity and health, plus she was viewed as a powerful protectress. She, along with Isis, is the patron goddess of Motherhood.

When Sacred Cow appears in a reading, your finances are about to improve or you could experience an unexpected windfall. Along with financial improvement comes increased prosperity. The Sacred Cow can represent a business deal or investment that will pay off well for you, especially if you see the card combination of Fish + Sacred Cow, with Fish representing money or finances in general and Sacred Cow indicating an increase of cash flow or something paying off well for you.

Sacred Cow also represents the Divine Feminine through its intimate association with the goddess Hathor. Therefore, when Sacred Cow appears in a reading, it can represent your mother, mother-in-law, an older woman who is a motherly figure, or a woman who is nurturing and caring toward others.

The goddess Hathor could also be a fierce protectress; therefore, when Sacred Cow appears in a reading, the card may indicate that you are under strong protection, either from an older woman or perhaps from some aspect of the Goddess Herself.

INTERPRETATIONS OF THE CARDS

SACRED COW:

ANCIENT EGYPTIAN MEANING

Cattle was very important in ancient Egypt as a source of food and milk. Owning cattle was a sign of great wealth and status. Cattle bones are found in tombs, along with other food items as examples of the importance of beef in the ancient Egyptian diet.

The cow was venerated as an animal representing Hathor and many of Her temples kept cows and saved them for important sacrifices. Bulls were also sacred, but to the god Osiris, and some bulls were actually mummified and buried as a form of offering.

Although a number of deities were associated with the cow (Nut of The Stars card was another, for one example), Hathor was the most popular. She was usually depicted as a woman with either the head of a cow, having cow ears, or as a full-bodied cow, with or without stars on her body.

Hathor is the goddess of joy, laughter, love, motherhood, prosperity, and abundance. She is seen as the source of all good things, a fertility goddess, and goddess of agriculture. Originally worshipped in the form of a cow with stylized stars on the body (as shown on this card), later depictions of Hathor evolved into a woman with the ears or head of a cow. Associated also with death and the underworld, the goddess Hathor was also viewed as a goddess of rebirth.

CARD 16 | STARS

Keywords: Success, Imagination, Wishes, Divination, Esoteric Studies, Guidance

Playing Card Association: 6 of Hearts (6H)

The Stars card in a reading is a positive card to receive. Depending on the type of question you ask, The Stars can indicate you are about to meet with success concerning a current endeavor. When asking questions about work, for instance, The Stars indicates that your boss or supervisor looks upon you favorably. When in doubt about how something may turn out, The Stars indicates a successful conclusion to the matter.

The Stars also indicates creativity and imagination. As an artist, I receive The Stars often in readings I do for myself and I usually take it to mean my artistic ability or creative urges. The Stars can represent an imaginative person who comes up with creative approaches and solutions to problems.

In some cases, The Stars can represent divination in terms of doing readings in order to seek answers or guidance. Connected strongly to the field of Astronomy, The Stars can indicate a person who is some type of scientist or it can represent the Sciences in general, as in a course of study in school.

The Stars also represents receiving guidance. The guidance can come from parents, teachers, friends, and even spiritual sources, such as dreams, intuition, or messages from your own angels and spirit guides.

STARS:
ANCIENT EGYPTIAN MEANING

The ancient Egyptians saw the body of the goddess Nut representing the nighttime sky as she arched across the heavens. The body of the goddess Nut adorns the ceilings of tombs and is depicted in *The Book of the Dead*. Her body not only represents the

INTERPRETATIONS OF THE CARDS

nighttime sky, but also the stellar location of the Duat, the Egyptian underworld. Nut's body is covered with a myriad of stars; as such, the outline of her body and her facial features blend into the very sky itself.

Nut is the goddess of the sky. In earlier times she was viewed as a mother goddess who gave birth to all the stars, in addition to the deities Isis, Osiris, Nephthys, and Set. Nut was also considered to be the mother of both the sun and the moon. Her husband is Geb, the god of earth. Like Hathor, Nut was also seen embodied in the cow and is sometimes depicted as a white cow with stars covering her body.

I chose to depict the Giza Plateau and the Nile River with the body of Nut arched overhead as the Milky Way. There is a controversial theory that the pyramids and Sphinx of the Giza Plateau are actually much older than what mainstream archaeologists believe. There has been no significant rainfall on the Giza Plateau that would result in any type of erosion since at least 10,500 B.C., yet it is widely known that the Sphinx has evidence of erosion all over its body; this is the type of erosion that is only produced by rainwater (Schoch, 1999).

Subsequent research and analysis of the Giza Plateau alignments by Bauval and Gilbert (1995), using computer programs that follow the orientation of constellations, mapped out the nighttime sky over the Giza Plateau as it would have looked at the time of the last significant rainfall in 10,500 BC. He discovered that the three pyramids of the Giza Plateau (the Great Pyramid of Khufu and the smaller pyramids of Khafre and Menkaure) aligned exactly with the three stars of Orion's Belt, as the constellation of Orion was directly overhead the Giza Plateau at that time. The Nile River at that time lined up with the Milky Way.

Bauval and Hancock (1995) discovered that the Sphinx was oriented to face eastward toward the constellation of Leo. It has long been argued that, originally, the Sphinx did not have the carved head of a man, but had a much larger carved head of a lion. The alignment of the Sphinx at 10,500 B.C. to the constellation of Leo to the east of Giza toward, which the Sphinx faced at that time, is compelling evidence that the small and out-of-proportion head of the Sphinx was actually that of a lion thousands of years ago that was then later carved into a smaller size to depict the pharaoh, Khephre.

For this card, I chose to depict the Giza Plateau as it would have looked in 10,500 B.C., with the alignments between the pyramids and Orion's Belt, and the Nile River with the Milky Way being emphasized. The body of the goddess Nut then stretches across the stellar landscape as not only the nighttime sky, but as the Milky Way itself.

CARD 17 | IBIS

Keywords: Change, Movement, Relocation

Playing Card Association: Queen of Hearts (QH)

Ibis is the animal I chose to represent the more traditional Storks card of the Lenormand. The Ibis was not only sacred in ancient Egypt, but it's meaning to the ancient Egyptians very much mirrored the meaning of the Stork to European users of Lenormand.

When Ibis appears in a reading, it can indicate something is about to change. What will change or what type of change is signified by the card that follows Ibis in the reading. For example, if you receive the card combination Ibis + Heart, followed by Ring, this would indicate a change in a relationship (Heart) and Ring would represent a firmer commitment, perhaps even marriage. When Ibis represents change, it's very important to take into account the surrounding cards to figure out what change is coming and how it will affect the situation.

Ibis can also represent movement in a situation. This is in terms of the situation developing and evolving. The movement represented by Ibis can be in either a positive or negative direction. Surrounding cards will give you additional clues.

INTERPRETATIONS OF THE CARDS

If you're asking about work and what to expect concerning your job, the Ibis paired with Anchor (steady work) or Fish (money) can indicate a coming promotion or raise.

IBIS:

ANCIENT EGYPTIAN MEANING

In ancient Egypt, the Ibis was sacred to the god Thoth, who is often depicted as a man with the head of an ibis. He was also closely associated with the baboon and can be found depicted in full baboon form with a lunar crescent on his head. Thoth is a lunar deity and he appears in the The Moon card as a man with the head of an ibis.

Thoth is the god responsible for giving humankind knowledge of the Sciences. He is a great Teacher and even the other gods consider him wise and would go to him with their problems—and Thoth would come up with a solution. He was referred to by the ancient Greeks as "Thrice-Great-Hermes" who was believed responsible for writing the esoteric treatise known as the Hermetica. Thoth is the god of wisdom and is closely associated with all educational pursuits.

CARD 18 | THE DOG

Keywords: Faithfulness, Loyalty, Fidelity, Friendship, Protection, Guidance, Trustworthy

Playing Card Association: 10 of Hearts (10H)

The Dog is a positive card that indicates someone close to you who is loyal and faithful. The Dog can represent a friend who is trustworthy. Paired with Heart, the Dog indicates fidelity in a romantic relationship. Next to a card representing a person, the Dog always points to this person as a friend, someone you can count on.

Dogs are known to protect their masters and guard their homes. When the Dog appears in a reading, it can mean that you or the subject of your question is protected. Dogs are also faithful companions and have helped many a lost person find their way back to their fellow humans. You often hear stories of someone lost in the woods, but their dog was able to help them find their way back home. Therefore, when Dog appears in a reading, this card can represent guidance.

DOG:
ANCIENT EGYPTIAN MEANING

Here we have a depiction of the god Anubis. He is more commonly known today by his Greek name, but to the ancient Egyptians, he was known as Anpu. Anubis is often depicted in art as a black man with the head of a black desert dog. He is a god of embalming, overseeing the embalming process the priests would undertake with the bodies of the deceased. Anubis was also seen as a guide for the soul during its perilous journey through the Duat, or underworld, on its way to rebirth as one of the countless stars. In his role as guide of the soul, Anubis was also seen as a protector.

Here, on this card, Anubis stands guard in the courtyard of the Temple of Isis at Philae, which is also the architectural feature in the Pharaoh and Priestess cards.

INTERPRETATIONS OF THE CARDS

CARD 19 | OBELISK

Keywords: Authority, Organizations, Government, Rules, Conformity, Status Quo

Playing Card Association: 6 of Spades (6S)

The Obelisk in other Lenormand decks is known as the Tower card. Here, I chose to depict it in keeping with the Egyptian theme. The obelisk, to the ancient Egyptians, carried the same connotations as the Tower for th Europeans.

Obelisk represents governmental record-keeping and, in ancient Egypt, the accomplishments of the pharaoh were carved onto the four sides of the structure. It was a tool for governmental propaganda. When this card appears in a reading, it can therefore represent the actual government, or a governmental institution; such as the IRS and CIA. In general, the Obelisk indicates an authority figure, so this could even point to a parent, teacher, supervisor, or boss.

The Obelisk can represent organizations, such as those mentioned above, but also any type of organized group of people who carry out group activities according to particular guidelines or rules. So, Obelisk can represent a school or church organization.

The Obelisk card is about following the rules, going along with the status quo and conforming to the way the group handles a situation, or conforming to their type of behavior.

OBELISK:

ANCIENT EGYPTIAN MEANING

An Obelisk was a four-sided structure with a pyramidal form at the summit. It was slightly tapered as you moved toward the top in order to help the base remain more secure.

Obelisks were erected between pylons in order to steady them so they wouldn't fall over. They were covered with hieroglyphic inscriptions on all four sides with the name of the pharaoh displayed prominently numerous times within a name cartouche, so the name would stand out among the rest of the glyphs. The text carved into obelisks would always focus on the great accomplishments of the pharaoh, although the vast majority of the text could not be read due to the obelisks standing so high.

INTERPRETATIONS OF THE CARDS

CARD 20 | GARDEN

Keywords: Socializing, Social Media, Parties, Gatherings, Groups, Concerts

Playing Card Association: 8 of Spades (8S)

The Garden is a place where family and friends can gather in order to socialize. Therefore, when Garden appears in a reading, it can mean just that: socializing with family and/or friends. Garden in a reading represents a gathering of people. When Garden appears next to Bouquet, it can indicate an invitation to a party. It can also represent groups, such as clubs.

In this modern day of online chatting and such, the Garden often appears in a reading to represent social media, but only if you yourself actively participate in social media or it somehow relates to your question.

The Garden can also represent just having a good time in general and going out, getting away from the house and work for a while in order to enjoy yourself.

GARDEN:

ANCIENT EGYPTIAN MEANING

As in modern times, the garden in ancient Egypt was a place where the family would gather with their friends and loved ones. Games would be played and, many times, meals would be eaten outside in the garden. It was a place of both fun and relaxation, much as it remains today for us all.

CARD 21 | MOUNTAIN

Keywords: Obstacles, Delays, Problems, Enemies, Goals, Aspirations

Playing Card Association: 8 of Clubs (8C)

When Mountain appears in a reading, it indicates you have something you need to surmount. Whether this is a problem, an obstacle, or some other issue, you need to find a way through or around it in order to achieve your goal. Mountain indicates difficult barriers standing between you and your desires that you will need to work through, which can cause delays. Therefore, Mountain also can represent delays to a situation, sometimes *very long* delays of up to a year or more can be indicated.

When it is near other negative cards, or a person card, Mountain can indicate the presence of an enemy. This person will wish for you to fail and may be purposely doing things or setting situations into motion that are all aimed at sabotaging you. When Mountain appears, it is important to look at surrounding cards. For example, when Mountain appears with Snake, this represents a powerful and malicious enemy who

INTERPRETATIONS OF THE CARDS

may be an older woman. Mountain with Desert Fox is an enemy who is skilled at lying and manipulating others.

Mountain can also indicate your goals or aspirations, if no other negative cards are nearby or any cards that may suggest Mountain is a delay. However, I've rarely seen this meaning for Mountain come up in a reading, but it is possible.

MOUNTAIN:
ANCIENT EGYPTIAN MEANING

The drawing here is of an actual mountain, Al-Qurn, that overlooks the Valley of the Kings, located near ancient Thebes, now modern-day Luxor. The Valley of the Kings was located along the western bank of the Nile. For the ancient Egyptians, the direction of west was symbolic of death. Today, the mountain goes by its Arabic name, Al-Qurn, but in ancient times it was known as "Dehent," The Horn. Dehent was a sacred site in the worship of the goddesses Hathor and Meretseger ("She Who Loves Silence") (Parsons 1996-2012). Some scholars believe the Valley of the Kings was chosen as the necropolis of the ruling class due to the resemblance of the shape of the mountain to the pryramidal form.

CARD 22 | CROSSROADS

Keywords: Choices, Alternatives, Decisions

Playing Card Association: Queen of Diamonds (QD)

This card is also known in other Lenormand decks as "Paths" and "Roads." In all decks I have seen this card is always depicted as two roads or paths intersecting.

Crossroads in a reading indicates that a choice needs to be made. You need to decide which way to go regarding the situation in question. Crossroads may indicate that you are faced with a number of alternatives from which to choose. A decision may be difficult, especially if Mice are nearby (meaning you are very worried about which alternative to choose) or Mountain (you're viewing the need to make a choice as a huge obstacle).

CROSSROADS: ANCIENT EGYPTIAN MEANING

For many who practice magic, the crossroads is a meeting place between this world and the world of spirit. Practitioners of various forms of magic will go to a nearby crossroads to commune with the spirits or they may bury things at the crossroads as offerings. This practice may be as ancient as Egypt itself, or even older. There is a pose in Egyptian art known as the "crossroads pose." The figure is shown with its right hand pointing up to the heavens and its left hand being held parallel to the horizon. Scholars have hypothesized that ancient Egyptians saw the crossroads as the meeting place between the spiritual realm and manifest reality (Imhotep, 2012). We may never know if the crossroads was considered the link between the two realms, but I find this concept interesting and definitely worthy of further scholarly research.

Interpretations of the Cards

CARD 23 | MICE

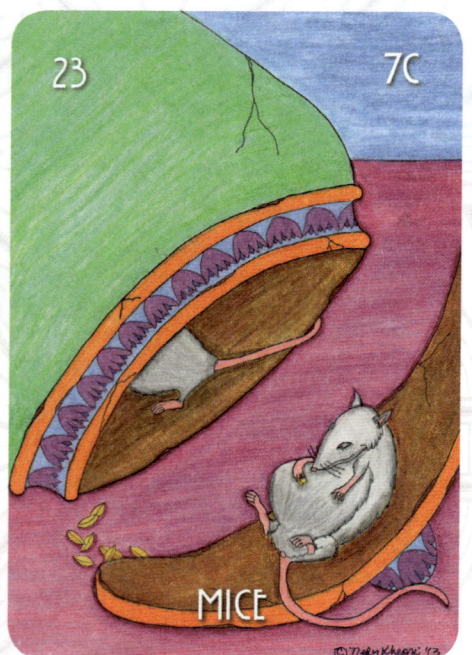

Keywords: Worry, Anxiety, Fear, Loss, Theft, Grief

Playing Card Association: 7 of Clubs (7C)

Mice is not a pleasant card. When the Mice card appears in a reading, it can indicate that something is eating away at you bit by bit. Mice says that you, or the person you are reading for, is very worried or fearful about something to the point that it may be causing them to suffer the symptoms of anxiety, which can include the inability to eat or sleep properly, headaches, and upset stomach. Mice in a reading can indicate that a person suffers from some type of anxiety disorder.

The appearance of Mice in a reading may indicate some form of loss or even theft. It can refer to an item that has been misplaced or something that has been taken by someone else. Usually, you will not find or get the item back. Due to their close association with loss, the Mice card can also represent grief or someone who is going through the grieving process over the loss of a loved one, or an extreme disappointment.

MICE:
ANCIENT EGYPTIAN MEANING

Mice were common throughout Egypt. The common house mouse (Mus musculus) was noted in *The Book of the Dead* (or, *The Book of Coming Forth By Day*, as it was known in ancient times) as "Ra's abomination" (Myasliwiec, 2000:202). They were seen as highly destructive.

The temple granaries were made of unbaked mud brick, so it was relatively easy for mice to burrow through the walls to get into the storage area. They were a real problem when it came to storing grain. This is why—despite the deity to whom they were dedicated—temples would be home to many cats. The cats helped to keep the mice population down so that the grain would not be completely destroyed.

Here, in this image, two Mice (or maybe more??) have managed to find, or even knock over, a vase used to store grain. They've gotten into it and only a few kernels remain. One little mouse has had her fill and rests on the lid of the vase, while the other mouse is greedily looking for more.

INTERPRETATIONS OF THE CARDS

CARD 24 | HEART

Keywords: Romance, Love, Affection, Compassion, Generosity

Playing Card Association: Jack of Hearts (JH)

The Heart card in a reading will represent your love life. Therefore, when using larger spreads it is important to examine all the surrounding cards because they will all give you additional details about your love life. In short, the Heart card represents romance, love—but just the feelings. It will not indicate a further commitment unless the Ring card follows because Ring represents commitment and partnership.

The Heart card can also represent great affection for someone or something, like the platonic love between best friends or your love of a hobby or job. The Heart, when near a person card, identifies them as being compassionate and generous. In matters of health, it represents the physical heart.

HEART:
ANCIENT EGYPTIAN MEANING

The Heart is known as the Ib in ancient Egyptian. I depicted a Valentine's Day-style heart at the center of this card; however, the Egyptians did not use this symbol. They used a stylized vase to represent the human heart, which is the item you see on the left side of the scale.

The Egyptians believed that the heart contained the soul, so when they would embalm a body, removing all the internal organs and placing them in Canopic jars, the heart would be left intact inside the body. It was believed if the heart was intact, the soul would be able to find its body and re-inhabit it in the spirit world. If the heart was harmed in any way, the soul would not be able to return to the body and would be incapable of experiencing spiritual rebirth.

The image on the card is of the Scales of Justice in the Duat, or underworld. The god of the dead, Osiris, would stand in judgment, while the god Thoth, god of knowledge and scribes, would read out the record of the deceased's life and their deeds. The heart was placed in the vase on the left and weighed against the Feather of Ma'at, the goddess of Divine Order and Justice. If a heart weighed more than Ma'at's feather, then there was a crocodile-like creature waiting to gobble it up, thus robbing the person of any chance of an afterlife and dooming them to roam in limbo for all eternity.

INTERPRETATIONS OF THE CARDS

CARD 25 | RING

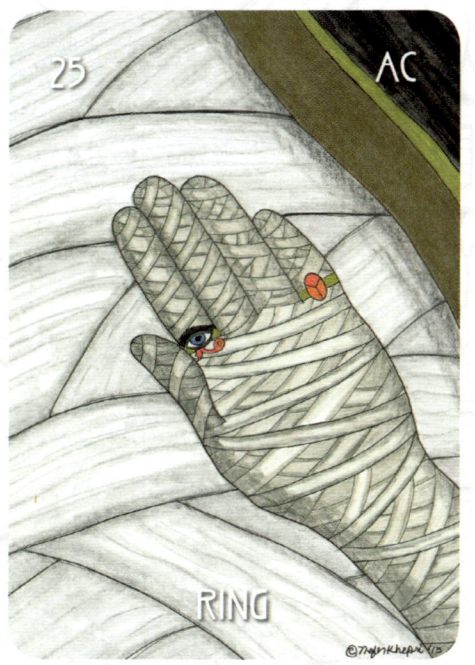

Keywords: Commitment, Partnership, Marriage, Business Deals, Legal and Binding Contracts

Playing Card Association: Ace of Clubs (AC)

    The Ring represents a commitment. It can be the obvious, which would be marriage, and, paired with Bouquet, it means an engagement. However, there are other types of important commitments to consider when the Ring card appears in a reading. The Ring basically signifies a committed relationship, whether it is romantic, business, or otherwise. The Ring can also signify business deals, or coming to an important agreement on something with another person. It can denote the signing of contracts of any type that are legal and binding, thus committing you to carry through with the contract.

RING:
ANCIENT EGYPTIAN MEANING

Rings were very popular jewelry in Egypt, just as they are today. The four most popular symbols that appeared on rings in ancient Egypt were the ankh, the scarab, the Eye of Ra, and the Eye of Horus, among other symbols. The Ankh signified life and breath. It also represented health and all manner of blessings. The scarab represented the god Khepera who pushed the sun across the sky each day, just as beetles would push around balls of dung that the Egyptians would see in their daily life.

The Eye of Ra and the Eye of Horus are two very important symbols of spiritual protection that many still use to this day, known collectively as the Wadjet. The Eye of Ra is personified as feminine solar power in the warrior goddess Sekhmet, predominantly, as well as other goddesses with strong solar associations, such as Hathor, Mut, and Bastet. At various points of Egyptian history, all of these goddesses carried the epithet of "The Eye of Ra."

The Eye of Ra as Sekhmet would smote the enemies of Ra, the Father of the Gods, and, in art and jewelry, is represented as the left eye. The god Horus (son of Isis and Osiris), in his epic battle against his uncle, the god Set, lost his right eye in the fight. The god Thoth replaced his eye with the moon and the right eye of Horus became the other Wadjet, or sacred eye amulet. In some versions of the same myth, it is said that Horus lost his left eye, so there is some disagreement in the ancient texts. Due to the eye of Horus being restored by Thoth, the Eye of Horus is also associated with healing and heka, the ancient Egyptian word for magic.

INTERPRETATIONS OF THE CARDS

CARD 26 | SCROLL

Keywords: Knowledge, Secrets, Education, Occult

Playing Card Association: 10 of Diamonds (10D)

    The Scroll card in other Lenormand decks is known as The Book. The ancient Egyptians did not have books as the Europeans understood them. They wrote on papyrus and would either roll up the text or they would attach numerous sheets together in a codex style that would then be folded accordion-style and stored in a box or a long vase.

    When the Scroll appears in a reading, you know one of two things: either there is some knowledge being imparted to you or there is a secret you need to figure out. The Scroll is a directional card like The Clouds and Sickle. If the Scroll represents a secret, then the rolled up portion of the scroll will be facing your significator card in a larger spread. So if your card is to the left of the Scroll, this card is talking about a secret. However, if your significator card lands to the right of the Scroll in the direction of the unfurled page, then this card represents some knowledge or perhaps a realization.

The type of knowledge represented by the Scroll ranges from something coming to your awareness, to education, to a spiritual realization. Surrounding cards will help to clarify what type of knowledge this card represents. For example, if you receive Scroll and the Obelisk is nearby, the Obelisk can represent institutions, such as schools and universities, so that combination would indicate knowledge gained through education. However, if the Stars is near the Scroll then the knowledge will be of a more esoteric nature and may come to you through divination.

Regarding secrets, this would indicate some knowledge or information of which you are unaware.

For the exposed sheet of this papyrus scroll, I chose the symbol of the Wadjet, or Eye of Horus, the right eye he lost in his fight with the god Set. The second symbol is known as the Shen, a glyph that depicts the sun resting on the horizon line. Both symbols represent protection.

SCROLL:
ANCIENT EGYPTIAN MEANING

Here, on this card, I tried to illustrate the crisscross weave of a sheet of papyrus paper. When you examine a sheet of papyrus, even modern papyrus upon which Egyptian-style paintings are done, you can see the weave of the fibers of the papyrus plant.

INTERPRETATIONS OF THE CARDS

CARD 27 | LETTER

Keywords: Letters, Paperwork, Email, Text, Fax, Documents, Mail/Post

Playing Card Association: 7 of Spades (7S)

The Letter represents written communication in all the forms it can take today, including electronic and via text on cell phones. Depending on surrounding cards, you can glean what sort of written communication is being represented by The Letter card. Letter with Obelisk can indicate legal papers, something to do with the law or government, like your income tax return, for example. Letter with Scroll can represent a school or university diploma, or perhaps a term paper or report card. Letter and Rider indicates you have some important mail soon to arrive.

LETTER:
ANCIENT EGYPTIAN MEANING

The Letter in this image is based on an actual glyphic inscription on papyrus (Pitt, 2011). I hand-drew it. The wonderful thing about papyrus is that it preserves well in the dry desert environment of Egyptian tombs. As a result, we have many glyphic inscriptions to study, in addition to what was carved onto the walls of tombs and temples.

Behind the letter on the card image is a long wooden plank that scribes would use as their palette. Words were written in black or red ink, so both paints were included on the scribe's palette. Brushes were carved from river reeds that are plentiful to this day in the delta region of the Nile River.

CARD 28 | GOD AND PHARAOH

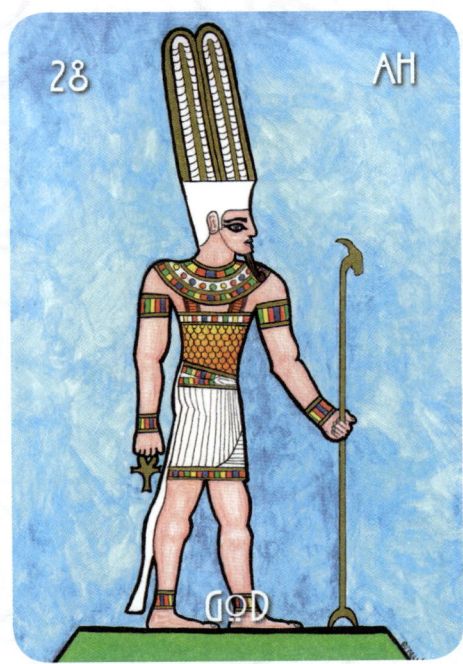

Keywords: A Man, Brother, Husband, Father, Uncle, Male Cousin or Friend

Playing Card Association: Ace of Hearts

There are two sets of male and female cards. When doing readings, you may wish to remove one set. Traditionally, Lenormand readings are done with only one of each, but, in modern times, deck designers take into account same-sex relationships.

I included two versions of what are called the Man and Woman or Gentleman and Lady cards in other Lenormand decks. The Man card, in *The Egyptian Lenormand* is The God and The Pharaoh. These two cards represent a male. Surrounding cards should identify him to you if he was not a part of your initial question for your reading. Keep in mind that the God and Pharaoh cards can represent you in the situation, if you are male. This card can be chosen for a male significator card to represent a man in the situation.

INTERPRETATIONS OF THE CARDS

GOD:

ANCIENT EGYPTIAN MEANING

For this card, I depicted the god, Amun-Ra. He is a combination of the gods Amun and Ra. Amun has been there since the beginning and is responsible for creating reality and all the other gods. Ra is the sun. Combined, Amun-Ra is the most powerful of all the gods. He is known as the father or king of all the gods. His animal counterpart was the ram, and the horns of the ram represented male virility. He was also depicted in full human form and, in rare cases, also as a goose, like the earth god, Geb, husband of Nut. Amun-Ra was considered to be pharaoh's father and protector. He rose to prominence in the 11th century B.C. and soon was considered the most powerful of all the gods.

PHARAOH:

ANCIENT EGYPTIAN MEANING

For the second Man card I created, I chose to depict the man as a Pharaoh. He wears a cloth headdress and stands to the left of his high priestess who is depicted on the Priestess card. The location I chose for this card is the courtyard of the Temple of Isis at Philae. When you place the Priestess and Pharaoh cards side by side, the Pharaoh and his Priestess stand together in the temple courtyard in front of the pylons of the temple. The Temple of Isis at Philae is also the main architectural feature in The Dog card. I originally created the Pharaoh and Priestess cards as a fitted pair.

CARD 29 |
GODDESS AND PRIESTESS

Keywords: A Woman, Mother, Wife, Sister, Female Friend or Relative

Playing Card Association: Ace of Spades

Like the male counterpart of God and Pharaoh, the Goddess and Priestess cards are simply interpreted as representing a female. Examine surrounding cards to identify the woman who may be represented. Keep in mind this card can appear to represent you in a reading, if you are female. This card can be chosen for a female significator card.

GODDESS:

ANCIENT EGYPTIAN MEANING

The Goddess card is a depiction of Queen Nefertari (1290–1254 B.C.E.) as the goddess Isis. Queen Nefertari was the wife of Rameses II, otherwise known

INTERPRETATIONS OF THE CARDS

as Rameses the Great. This rendition is based upon a painting of Nefertari that is in her tomb. It is predominantly from Isis that I channeled these images. Isis is known by many epithets, including Queen of Heaven, She of 10,000 Names (for Isis is all Goddesses), Great Physician and Mistress of Healing, and She Who is Great of Magic, just to name a few.

According to Plutarch (1970), Isis was a devoted wife to the god Osiris, and when He was murdered by their brother Set, Isis searched the world for her husband's dismembered body parts. She knew that the sun god Ra had the power to raise the dead, something Isis was unable to do. So, She tricked Ra into giving Her His real name. Names have great power. Once she had Ra's true name, She had access to His power. She was then able to resurrect Osiris, but He had to live in the Underworld as ruler of the dead. The stealing of Ra's true name is how Isis became She Who is Great of Magic.

PRIESTESS:
ANCIENT EGYPTIAN MEANING

Priestesses were normally of noble blood, usually the younger daughters of Pharaoh whose marriages would never bring him any political alliance worth considering because the youngest daughter was far removed from the throne. Consequently, young daughters were often sent to serve the gods in the temples. A title popular during the New Kingdom was "Gods Wife of Amun" (Parsons, 2011).

CARD 30 |
WATER LILY

Keywords: Satisfaction, Peace, Harmony, Wisdom, Maturity, Family, Safety, Sex

Playing Card Association: King of Spades (KS)

    This card is called Lily or Lilies in other Lenormand decks. I named mine Water Lily and chose to illustrate a lotus flower because they were sacred to the ancient Egyptians. The lotus is a member of the Lily family, and, for the Egyptians, the lotus had the same meanings as the Lily does to European users of the Lenormand.

    When the Water Lily appears in a reading it can represent an older mature person, usually a man, but not always. The Water Lily points to someone who is wise due to their life experience, so that implies they are also older.

    Water Lily can represent peace and harmony. When it appears in a reading, it may be telling you that things are flowing along smoothly and that you should be content with how things are going. It can also indicate safety and may be telling you that all involved are protected and you need not worry.

INTERPRETATIONS OF THE CARDS

Water Lily can represent the family, either immediate or extended. If House is next to Water Lily, then Water Lily will represent those family members with whom you share a home. Water Lily indicates a stable, happy family life.

Water Lily can also represent sex in a reading and can be a reference to your sex life. If next to Sun, for example, Water Lily would indicate a very active and mutually satisfying sex life for you and your partner. However, if Water Lily is next to Whips, that can indicate S&M or other sexual practices that don't fall within the status quo. It will depend upon your question as to the determination that Water Lily is talking about sex or one of its other references.

My husband was quick to realize something totally unintentional about this card. If you look at the shadow of the Water Lily cast into the water, it takes the form of an angel. I work closely with Archangel Michael, who is the angel of the Blue Ray. I truly believe he has made his presence known in this card.

extending upward. The Water Lily lotus closes up at night and descends into the water only to rise again the next day. Based upon its behavior, the Water Lily lotus was connected to cosmic creation, the sun, and rebirth. It was believed that on the first day of creation the flower rose from the primordial water and, from its center, rose the sun for the very first time. It was the official flower of Upper Egypt.

The ancient Egyptians viewed the Water Lily lotus as representing spiritual enlightenment, healing (a health tonic was made from it and it also had hallucinogenic properties), and it was used in many herbal remedies. The Water Lily lotus was also connected to sexuality and was used in wooing women. It represented fertility, rebirth, and the afterlife.

WATER LILY:
ANCIENT EGYPTIAN MEANING

The Water Lily, or lotus flower, was held very sacred. It is the only flower that simultaneously fruits and flowers. It grows in muddy swamps and extends up from the water, having fifteen oval, spreading petals with the center a flat seed pod and stamens

CARD 31 | SUN

Keywords: Success, Victory, Achievement, Glory, Charm

Playing Card Association: Ace of Diamonds (AD)

When The Sun appears in a reading, it is a card of great success and of perhaps gaining some renown through your success. You may be the focus of the respect and admiration of others for your achievements.

People who appear in readings with The Sun card are charming and charismatic. They have natural sunny dispositions, are cheerful and friendly.

The Sun can represent having the determination to overcome adversity, despite the obstacles you may be facing. The Sun represents summertime and hot environments, such as the desert.

INTERPRETATIONS OF THE CARDS

SUN:

ANCIENT EGYPTIAN MEANING

The sun was venerated as a god in ancient Egypt. Known as Ra and Khepera, the sun was considered the source of all life, even of the other gods. The sun was life-giving and life-sustaining, the source of all that was considered benevolent. The worship of the sun was the center of life and the sun was seen as the center of the universe.

The sun was of such tremendous importance to the Egyptians that during the Amarna Period in the 18th Dynasty, when the heretic pharaoh, Akenaten, sought to dissolve Egyptian religion and create a monotheistic state religion, the sun still was held supreme. Akenaten claimed to be the son of the sun and he called the sun "Aten." Nobility of the period used "Aten" as the suffix to their name, as in Akenaten. The priests of Ra and Amun lost all their power under Akenaten as he worked to dissolve the temples and take the temple riches for himself. However, immediately after his death, normality was restored under Tutankhamun, as the cult of the god Amun-Ra was re-established.

The image on this card has a giant beetle pushing the sun up higher into the sky. The beetle was known as the god Khepera and he would roll the sun across the sky daily. The beetle was in reality the dung beetle and the Egyptians would see these beetles frequently pushing around balls of dung in which they would lay their eggs.

CARD 32 | MOON

Keywords: Recognition, Fame, Honors, Imagination, Dreams, Creativity

Playing Card Association: 8 of Hearts (8H)

The Moon is one of the cards Lenormand readers choose as the Work card in a deck. Personally, I see the Anchor as the work card, but I leave it up to the users of my deck which card they prefer to assign to the life category of Work. Just keep in mind you can only do this with one card. Another choice for the work card that many use is the Desert Fox. So, decide which it is for you and then stick to that.

When Moon rises in a reading, it indicates something you have done, or are about to do, has called the attention of others. Usually, it denotes some type of project or achievement that others will look favorably upon. Thus, it will gain you some recognition and, perhaps down the road, even fame and honors. The Moon can also represent the honors that students receive or a good employee who is rewarded with a raise or a promotion.

The Moon can also represent creativity, especially artistic creativity and it can represent an artistic person in your reading. It is also connected to the field of entertainment—singing, acting, writing, and so on.

The Moon card of the Lenormand does not have the same interpretation as the Moon of the Tarot. For those of you who also read Tarot, please keep this in mind.

MOON:

ANCIENT EGYPTIAN MEANING

The moon was also venerated as a god in ancient Egypt—but not to the great extent that the sun was—that had an entire cult devoted to its worship. The Moon was seen as female, but—like the sun—it has both female and male gods associated with it. One of the chief lunar deities was Thoth, the god of Knowledge and Science. According to legend, when the god Horus lost his eye in a fight with the god Set, it is said Thoth took the moon and used it to replace the missing eye of Horus.

INTERPRETATIONS OF THE CARDS

CARD 33 | KEY

Keywords: Success, Mastery, Solution, Opportunity, Fate/Destiny, Karma

Playing Card Association: 8 of Diamonds (8D)

The Key in a reading can unlock and open doors, but it can also serve to lock them. Look to surrounding cards to see if Key is an opener or a closer. When Key appears with other positive cards, it usually means the matter will resolve successfully or could be pointing you in the direction of new opportunities that you may have otherwise overlooked.

The Key can indicate a major event, something that may be life-changing. Due to this association, it is seen by some readers as representing Fate, Destiny, and/or Karma.

The Key indicates a successful solution if you are asking about a problem you or someone else is experiencing. The Key says that things will work out for a positive outcome.

KEY:
ANCIENT EGYPTIAN MEANING

The ancient Egyptians did not have keys—skeleton or otherwise. However, I wanted to maintain the look of a key while still incorporating an Egyptian style, so I kept the toothy end of the Key while adding an Ankh as the handle. The Ankh symbolizes breath, life, blessings, and was carried by gods in Egyptian artwork as a symbol of not only their power, but also of their ability to confer life or remove it at whim.

CARD 34 | FISH

Keywords: Money, Business, Trade, Entrepreneurship, Abundance, Prosperity, Increase

Playing Card Association: King of Diamonds (KD)

I read the Lenormand Fish as the money card. Sacred Cow can indicate a raise, windfall, or finances in general, but it is the Fish that represents physical money and prosperity. Fish can also mean increase in general; as a result, it's a very positive card—as long as it's shown to be increasing good things.

The Fish can appear in readings about business or running a business. This is about small businesses, not huge corporations or companies. These will be represented by the Obelisk card. Fish, when it comes to business, is about businesses that are run by entrepreneurs who are self-made people. They have created their business from nothing and they do what they can to help it to grow. When next to House, Fish will indicate a business that is run out of the home.

Fish in a reading can also appear when representing the need to do your best and pull yourself up by your own bootstraps. This card is a sign for you not to allow the circumstances to

INTERPRETATIONS OF THE CARDS

keep you down. It's encouraging you to improve your outlook and think more positively.

FISH:

ANCIENT EGYPTIAN MEANING

Fish was important to ancient Egyptians. It was fished out of the Nile and the Mediterranean as a source of food and was also used as fertilizer for the crops. Fish are depicted on tomb walls and in other Egyptian art.

The fish I show here is the Nile River Tilapia, indigenous to the Nile River to this day. I could have chosen a much prettier fish. Carp is commonly chosen by artists to depict The Fish card (as I did for my contribution to the group Lenormand deck, *Le Petit Lenormand Electique* (2012), but for this deck, I decided to use an indigenous fish that was an important source of food and fertilizer in ancient, as well as, modern times.

The tilapia fish in particular, for the ancient Egyptians, symbolized regeneration and rebirth (Wegner, 2011). Most likely this belief was connected to their use as fertilizer to help with the growth of crops.

CARD 35 | ANCHOR

Keywords: Stability, Slow Progress, Plans, Inheritance/Legacy, Determination, Safety

Playing Card Association: 9 of Spades (9S)

    The Anchor is another card that can represent Work, and, personally, this is the card I use to represent Work in my Lenormand readings. Other choices traditionally used to represent Work are the Moon and Desert Fox. Choose one and stick to it for your own readings.

    When the Anchor appears in your reading, it indicates that whatever the surrounding cards represent, things are stable and secure. The Anchor can mean that things are moving slowly in a situation, but not nearly as slowly as what Mountain would indicate. Sometimes things are meant to move forward slowly and the presence of Anchor in a reading may indicate slow progress, but still progress nonetheless.

    The Anchor can represent making plans or the need to do so. You may need to map out a plan of approach to a specific situation in order to assure eventual success. If near a money card, Anchor

INTERPRETATIONS OF THE CARDS

may indicate the need to create and stick to a monthly budget, especially if it comes up with Sacred Cow.

The Anchor, like Tree, grounds and stabilizes us. As such, it also represents inheritance or legacy through the family and this includes our ancestors, known and unknown.

Anchors help ships to stay in place, despite the currents of rivers, lakes, and the ocean. Therefore, Anchor helps us to remain secure, and also represents a source of determination and will power when it comes to the need to stand firm in your resolve.

ANCHOR:
ANCIENT EGYPTIAN MEANING

Anchors in ancient times were merely large limestone slabs roughly carved into tombstone-type or triangular shapes. A large hole was then drilled and carved into it through which a large thick rope would be attached in order to drop the anchor from the ship. A groove sometimes extended from above the hole to the edge on both sides into which the rope would rest (Galili, Sharvit, and Artzy, 1994:97). Some were carved with a symbol on their surfaces that was most likely the name of the ship to which they belonged. Size varied greatly, depending on the size of ship they were intended to anchor, with huge warships commanding the largest anchors, some as long as three feet and as thick as two feet.

CARD 36 | DJED PILLAR

Keywords: Grief, Burdens, Hardship, Responsibility, Unpleasantness, Guilt, Pain, Suffering

Playing Card Association: 6 of Clubs (6C)

This card in other Lenormand decks is depicted with a cross, and is called "Cross." The Egyptians did not have crosses (although it was a popular form of execution in ancient Rome). I chose a symbol and glyphic element known as the Djed Pillar for the Cross card because it carries the same connotations as the Lenormand Cross and it is also is in keeping with the ancient Egyptian theme of this deck.

Djed Pillar in a reading is never a good sign. It denotes those responsibilities of life that we see as burdens, but we must carry them through and fulfill our obligations. In this way, it represents the unpleasant things in life we have to deal with, like your annual dental cleaning or doing your income taxes.

However, Djed Pillar can also take on much more serious and upsetting meanings, such as carrying guilt forward through your life for something in the past that you did and have never been able to release. The Djed Pillar can also represent tremendous hardship,

INTERPRETATIONS OF THE CARDS

pain, and/or suffering. For example, if Djed Pillar appears in a reading next to Sarcophagus it can indicate a severe and painful illness that may result in death.

DJED PILLAR:

ANCIENT EGYPTIAN MEANING

The Djed Pillar represented the spine of the god Osiris, particularly the lumbar vertebrae. According to the myth, as told by Plutarch (1970), Set, the brother of Osiris, coveted the throne. He conspired to kill Osiris, but knowing of Isis' (the wife of Osiris) great powers of healing, Set decided to dismember the body of Osiris into fourteen pieces, one of which was his spine, which the Djed Pillar represents. In another story about the same fratricide, Set buries the body of Osiris in a tree and it is this tree that then becomes the Djed Pillar that Set later used as a pillar in his palace with the body of his murdered brother within it (Alm, 2012).

Isis mourned her beloved greatly and traveled the entire world gathering up all the pieces of her husband's body. She found them all, except the phallus, which was eaten by a fish. Yet, with the power she had tricked the old god Ra into giving her, Isis was able to resurrect her beloved and was somehow magically able to conceive Horus, who then grew to defeat his uncle Set in battle and win back the throne of Egypt.

For the ancient Egyptians, the Djed Pillar represented mourning, grief, hardship, and was also synonymous with the god, Osiris. Spell 155 of *The Book of the Dead* (to the Egyptians, *The Book of Coming Forth by Day*) (Faulkner 2005:177), states in a prayer that an amulet of the Djed Pillar was placed on the throat of the deceased to insure a place with the gods. The Djed Pillar is shown in many artistic examples from tombs and texts holding up the sky or heavens (Brown, 2002). What greater burden is there than that?

CARD 37 | CAT

Keywords: Intelligent, Aloof, Secretive, Playful, Territorial, Alertness

Playing Card Association: 10 of Hearts

If you are using both the Cat and Dog cards, the Cat will have the meaning listed here. In the case of using both cards in a reading, the Cat card does NOT mean the same thing as the Dog card. If you so desire, you may substitute the Cat card for the Dog card. In that case, Cat takes on the meaning of Dog and you will need to remove Dog from the deck for your reading.

When Cat pounces into your reading, she is calling your attention to whatever card falls before it. If it appears as the first card in your reading then choose the BOTTOM card of the deck and this will be what the Cat is trying to emphasize for you. Mainly, the Cat is telling you that you need to be alert to whatever is going on around you or the situation. The other cards will tell you what you should be alert for.

Cats are known to be aloof, and the Cat card can represent a person who is aloof or emotionally distant. Cats are also intelligent and the appearance of the Cat in a reading can represent a person of high intelligence or someone who has a firm grip on the situation

INTERPRETATIONS OF THE CARDS

under question. Cats are also very active creatures (when they're not busy sleeping), so it may represent a situation that is changing or evolving quickly; or, it can represent a person who moves gracefully, but with speed. Cats are secretive. We never know what our pet cats are thinking and the Cat card can represent the ability to play one's cards close to the vest, keep secrets, or be secretive.

CAT:

ANCIENT EGYPTIAN MEANING

The personality of the Chartreux (depicted on the left as my own cat, Bluestar) matches the meaning of this card perfectly. As with all cats, the Chartreux can be aloof, but they are very alert, active, and intelligent. They love to play, are fantastic mousers and ratters, and they can be very territorial of their homes and of their human owners, usually attaching to just one or two family members. The household tabby kitten represented in the center symbolizes all cats and their ability to add happiness to a home.

Egypt is often credited as the location where the cat was first domesticated as a household pet. Originally used for pest control because Egypt was badly infested with mice, the cat soon graduated to a beloved family pet to the point that many cats are found fully embalmed in Egyptian tombs. The British Museum in London, England, has a fine display case full of the mummies of cats from the tombs of Egypt.

The cat-headed goddess, Bastet, is depicted on this card. She is a goddess of love, happiness, and the home. In her angry aspect as the lion-headed goddess, Sekhmet, she is a goddess of war who does not believe in taking any prisoners.

THE LENORMAND "WORK" CARD

The Lenormand card that signifies "Work" to the reader depends upon which school of Lenormand a reader follows. The Work Card can be any one of these three cards:

The Desert Fox
traditionally: The Fox

The Moon

The Anchor

What every reader needs to do for themselves is to read the meanings of each of these three traditional Work cards, examine the imagery, and then decide which card will be *your* Work card. Once you have decided which of the three will represent "work" to you, maintain that card as your Work card. Do not switch back and forth, or this will lead to some very confusing readings.

Now, as to what your Work Card will cover, regardless of which Lenormand card you have chosen, it covers the following:

- Anything and everything concerning your job and/or career

- The work environment itself (office, farm, school, etc...)

- Employment

- Seeking a job/work

- "Working," as in the verb itself

THE DESERT FOX is known as the self-employment card. This card, especially when it comes along with House, means you work from home or that you are self-employed, although you may maintain an office or storefront away from your house. The Desert Fox is chosen as the work card because it is important to many to be intelligent and cunning in the workplace.

THE MOON is often chosen because it represents those things most people desire from their careers: fame and recognition.

INTERPRETATIONS OF THE CARDS

THE ANCHOR can also be chosen as a work card because people desire stability in their jobs and also a stable income.

The use of the Work card as a verb for "working" can sometimes appear in a reading. For example, let's say my Work Card is The Anchor (which it is), and I'm asking what can I do to strength my relationship with a good friend because I sense things are not as great as they once were and she is growing distant.

First of all, I have to include both female cards as I shuffle the deck (Goddess and Priestess) because I am asking about another woman. I choose the Goddess to represent myself and the Priestess to represent my friend.

Let's say I end up drawing Goddess + Desert Fox + Flowers + Priestess.

The Goddess is myself. Regarding Desert Fox, I at first think it represents deceit. So, to begin with, I would think some sort of deceit is going on, but then Flowers follows Fox, and that is a very positive card, meaning gift, happiness, and perhaps a pleasant exchange of some type. The Priestess would then represent my aloof friend.

I would then go back and deduce that Desert Fox does not represent deceit, but that if I want the relationship with my friend to "work out," or become stronger, then the advice is Flowers—give her a gift, show her how much she means to me.

In this case, the Desert Fox card is behaving like a verb for the relationship I'm asking about. In order to get this relationship to "work" (Desert Fox) I need to present my friend with a gift (Flowers).

I hope this clarifies how your Work Card will function in a reading and how it can also function as the verb "to work," "working", "will work," and "worked" —depending on its position in the spread.

LOCATION AND LENORMAND CARDS

Particular locations are associated with the Lenormand cards. However, Lenormand experts differ in their opinions of the locations signified by each card. Location associations are based upon two things: the traditional interpretation of the card and the imagery depicted on that particular card. For example, in many decks the Rider card is depicted as a man on a horse. In most, the horse is jumping over a low-lying fence in a grassy, sometimes wooded environment. In that case, someone could say that the Rider card represents grassy, sporadically wooded areas; however, in another deck, the Rider may be depicted on his horse traversing a mountain pass. In that case, the Rider card could be viewed as representing mountainous terrain and narrow restricted spaces. The examples of different renditions of the Rider card illustrate that the deck you are using will often determine your location associations for each of the Lenormand cards. Also, your own experiences and awareness of different environments and other places will play a large role in any location associations you may assign to particular cards.

As a result, I recommend you examine carefully the cards of your deck, and while taking the interpretations of each card into account, arrive at your own list of associated locations for each card. Be sure to write your list down for future reference.

Below are two examples of lists arrived at independently by myself and then together with one of my Lenormand students. Both lists are based upon the imagery of *The Egyptian Lenormand*. The first list is very basic and was done very quickly off the top of my head to demonstrate to my students how easy it is to arrive at your own location associations for the cards. The second example is much more specific and is based upon more specific personal experience and associations.

My own quick reference list is as follows—but by all means, please attempt to come up with your own location associations for each of the cards.

1. **RIDER:** along a road or highway

2. **CLOVER:** a yard

3. **SHIP:** over a body of water, an ocean

4. **HOUSE:** in a house

5. **TREE:** a physical tree, woods, forest, backyard (if there are trees located there)

6. **CLOUDS:** the sky, rainy, and/or wet environments

7. **SNAKE:** drains (as in plumbing), a place that is twisty (a long and winding road)

8. **SARCOPHAGUS:** funeral parlor, graveyard (this card in other decks is called Coffin)

9. **FLOWERS:** florist shop, gift shop

10. **SICKLE:** field, farm, ranch

11. **CROOK & FLAIL:** a court room or places where arguments occur

12. **BIRDS:** café, online chat rooms

13. **CHILD:** classroom, daycare, school

14. **DESERT FOX:** desert, dry environment, wilderness

15. **SACRED COW:** a bank or other financial institution (like the stock exchange)

75

INTERPRETATIONS OF THE CARDS

16. **STARS:** outer space, other planets, an observatory

17. **IBIS:** along a shoreline, low-lying water, possibly a pond

18. **DOG:** the pound, the vet's, a friend's house

19. **OBELISK:** any building that carries out governmental or educational business, classroom, hospital, large office building

20. **GARDEN:** public park

21. **MOUNTAIN:** mountainous area, a particular mountain range

22. **CROSSROADS:** an intersection of two roads, highways

23. **MICE:** cupboard, drawer, the floorboards, basement, attic (all places where mice like to hang out)

24. **HEART:** romantic meeting place (like Lover's Lane), a dark theater, the type of places where couples go to spend time together and make out

25. **RING:** justice of the peace's office, wedding chapel

26. **SCROLL:** school, university, library, bookstore

27. **LETTER:** post office

28./29. **GOD/DESS; PHARAOH/ PRIESTESS:** not applicable

30. **WATER LILY:** pond (either natural or man-made)

31. **SUN:** hot location, tropical, desert area

32. **MOON:** cold location, ice and snow

33. **KEY:** a lock, safe, safety deposit box (things that are locked)

34. **FISH:** lake, ocean, river, stream

35. **ANCHOR:** along the coastline, a beach

36. **DJED PILLAR:** church

37. **CAT:** animal clinic, pet store, animal shelter

According to Jessica Olson (personal communication, 2013) and I, additional location associations for the Lenormand cards based upon personal knowledge and experiences can be easily listed. I recommend once again that you do not depend on the lists here, but create your own that include your personal associations.

1. **RIDER:** desert climate, road trip, dry climate, mesa

2. **CLOVER:** prairie, fields, the American Midwest

3. **SHIP:** ocean cruise, dinner cruise, yachting, fishing, river ways, lakes, ponds, Great Lakes state or any country known for large water ways, Greece, Portugal, Spain

4. **HOUSE:** Condo, Cabin, Wisconsin, Canada, areas where cabins are prevalent

5. **TREE:** island vacation, California, Florida

6. **CLOUDS:** places where rain is known to be prevalent, rainy weather, storms, Seattle, London, England, etc…

7. **SNAKE:** mountain roads, desert areas, areas where spiders and scorpions reside, Africa, areas where there are many snakes

8. **SARCOPHAGUS:** Egypt, Transylvania, places of ancient history and mystery

9. **FLOWERS:** places where many Swedes and Fins reside or any other Scandinavians, Wisconsin, Minnesota, European countries

10. **SICKLE:** farm country, farming community, areas where commodities are the main source of income

11. **CROOK & FLAIL:** Middle Eastern countries, areas where middle eastern communities are prevalent, places that have strict laws and adherence to cultural practices

12. **BIRDS:** snow birds, people who migrate to a different area with changes of the seasons, seasonal workers, people who travel with a circus

13. **CHILD:** daycare center, Disneyland and Disney World, Six Flags, and other amusement parks, areas where children are catered to

14. **DESERT FOX:** areas with a dry climate

15. **SACRED COW:** investment institutes, stock market, Wall Street, and other iconic financial institutions

16. **STARS:** astral projection, ballooning, hang-gliding, parachuting

17. **IBIS:** watery environments (for example—the Florida Everglades)

18. **DOG:** breeders or any area where breeding is prevalent, kennel

19. **OBELISK:** locations where monuments are common (like Washington, D. C.; Capital building; capital of any country or state)

20. **GARDEN:** Georgia, concerts, oasis

21. **MOUNTAIN:** Colorado, the Andes, any mountainous area, mountain-climbing vacation, heights

22. **CROSSROADS:** undecided vacation spot, crossing many borders (like in mainland Europe, state-to-state or country-to-country)

23. **MICE:** depressing vacation, area of infestation

24. **HEART:** cardiac rehab, honeymoon, bridal suite of a hotel

25. **RING:** areas where marriages are held, wedding chapel

26. **SCROLL:** libraries, areas of study, Library of Congress or any country's equivalent

INTERPRETATIONS OF THE CARDS

27. LETTER: passport, letters of entry, tourist areas where writing is a prominent draw (as in the Hemingway estate)

28. GOD OR PHARAOH: churches, religious gatherings, Christian college, ancient Egypt

29. GODDESS OR PRIESTESS: female retreat, spa day

30. WATER LILY: ponds, day spa, peaceful holiday, nude beaches, singles getaway, adult only vacation spots, area of nightlife

31. SUN: sunny vacation spots: Mexico, Jamaica, Florida, Egypt, places where it is hot with many bugs, maybe swamp areas, camping in very warm and muggy weather

32. MOON: moonlit cruise, honeymoon, moonlit walk, night concert

33. KEY: condominium, passport, gateway

34. FISH: expensive trip or event, fishing trip, ocean fishing, diving vacation or trip, scuba class

35. ANCHOR: underwater monuments, Okinawa, Yonaguni, etc…

36. DJED PILLAR: places where there are strict or stringent laws and rules, Russia, communist countries, prisons, Alcatraz, areas where the Underground Railroad existed

37. CAT: places where cats are, Africa, kennels, zoos

   As you can see from the above lists, once you get to know your cards, it is fairly easy to associate each card to particular places. This should be based upon your own experience with traveling and what you know of other locations. Try not to adhere strictly to the associations here—come up with your own.

HOW TO READ LENORMAND CARDS

EXERCISE 1

Examine your deck and place the cards into 3 piles based on how the imagery makes you feel.

Pile 1: positive cards

Pile 2: neutral cards

Pile 3: negative cards

If any cards are difficult and you find you just can't decide, then place them into a fourth pile labeled "unknown", but try not to do this at all.

This will be an interesting exercise to undertake, especially if you know nothing of traditional Lenormand. The exercise will give you a good start as to being able to identify the overall energy of a reading once you start conducting them.

Make a list of the names of each card in each of your piles for future reference. Once you learn the meanings of the cards, you can then compare your list to the meanings to see how well your own choices correspond to the actual meanings of the cards.

Prior to attempting to do any actual readings, here are two very simple exercises you can do in order to become better acquainted with your cards.

EXERCISE 2

Examine each card—you can do this in or out of numerical order; it doesn't matter.

List 3–5 keywords you think may be associated with each card. Focus on the image, the colors used, and how the card makes you feel to come up with keywords.

As you examine each image, a good question to ask yourself is: "What does this image make me think of?" Another question you can ask yourself is, "How does this card make me feel?" Then write those answers down. Your keywords can be nouns or verbs.

How to Read Lenormand Cards

How to Use This Deck

When preparing to do a reading, ideally you should be in a quiet place where you won't be disturbed.

Breathe in and out deeply, emptying your lungs with each exhale and completely filling them with each inhale. Do this 3–7 times. This helps to center you and clear your mind.

Then decide on your question. Be clear and specific. The more specific your questions are phrased, the more accurate and direct your readings will be. You may wish to write your question down; for Lenormand readings—since the results can be so immediate—I do strongly recommend that you keep a journal for your readings. You can then go back to it later to see how accurate you've been or if maybe the cards meant something other than how you interpreted them.

Shuffle in a way that feels the most comfortable to you. My practice is to shuffle the cards 5 or 7 times; then I cut them into thirds and re-stack the deck, choosing the middle deck first, so that the cut pile in the center ends up the top of the reassembled deck. Every reader has their own way of shuffling. The choice is yours. There are no set "rules" as to how *The Egyptian Lenormand* is to be shuffled.

READING THE CUT

However, I do ask that you do one thing with every reading. Cut the cards and look at the cards on the bottom of each pile of cut cards. Some cut the cards just once, so you have two piles. Some, like myself, cut the deck into thirds, giving you three piles. What I then do before I reassemble the deck is I make a note of the bottom card of each pile.

I have noticed in my own Lenormand readings for myself and for clients that the cut is very important almost every single time. Examine the cards and whether you do a 2-pile or a 3-pile cut, take into account the card combinations as well. I have noticed that the cut tends to provide information of something unexpected or that occurs suddenly. It's never bad things, at least not yet, but things that are most likely not a part of your normal routine. Also, keep in mind if someone around you is planning a surprise, reading the cut may ruin it. This happened with a client of mine and her husband was kind of upset over it. Whether you read the cut of your cards or not is up to you, but I do highly recommend it.

Timing and the Lenormand

Many people wish to know *when* something will occur. There are timing cards in the Lenormand, but I do not discuss that here as that information can be found online and elsewhere (Steinbach, 2007). I do suggest that when you formulate your questions for your readings, if you are wishing for something to occur within a certain time frame, by all means, state the time frame as part of your question. For example, "What are the chances that I get a new car in the next 4 months?" If you get all negative cards or a reading that is noncommittal, ask your question using a different time frame. This method can then tell you exactly when something is most likely to occur, but you may have to throw several card spreads on the table before you arrive at your answer.

YES AND NO QUESTIONS

The Lenormand cards do not handle yes/no questions well. In order to avoid phrasing your question as a yes/no, you may wish to try this:

QUESTION: *Will I get promoted at work within the next 2 months? Yes or no?*

REPHRASED: *What are my chances of getting a promotion at work within the next two months?*

When you rephrase the question, you avoid the yes/no question construct completely and the Lenormand can deal with this type of question quite easily.

The word change is what alters the entire dynamic of your question—it is no longer a yes/no question. When you insert the word "chances" your question then becomes one of probability. Any type of divinatory system deals much better with probability than with concrete outcomes indicated by a yes/no question.

LENORMAND SYNTAX

In brief, Lenormand is easily read from left to right as you would read a book. The card on the left is the subject or noun card. The card to its right is the adjective card. It will give further information about the subject card.

When reading Lenormand, combinations are VERY important, as they can alter the entire meaning of a reading. Rather than looking at each card in isolation and interpreting it in that manner, with Lenormand you are meant to read the cards in pairs. This gives your readings an added dimension and depth.

There are two cardinal rules when reading Lenormand card combinations you must always keep in mind. They are as follows:

Card A is the subject card, while Card B is the adjective that gives you additional details about Card A. Reading Lenormand is very different from mathematics. A + B does NOT equal B + A.

Let's examine a few card combinations as examples.

How to Read Lenormand Cards

Scroll + Mountain tells you that the subject, Card A, Scroll, is about education, learning, perhaps even secrets, which are all meanings traditionally associated with that card.

Card B, Mountain, represents delays, obstacles, perhaps even the presence of a powerful enemy.

Read together, the Mountain card provides additional details about the Scroll card. Here, the card combination of Scroll + Mountain is telling you that your education, learning process, or perhaps a secret is going to be delayed, or there will be problems affecting education or learning. Scroll + Mountain may indicate that the sharing of a secret may cause problems.

Now, reversing that card combination you have: Mountain + Scroll. Here, the Scroll card is acting as an adjective to the Mountain card, which is now the subject of the card combination. In this case, Scroll can indicate knowledge coming to light about either a problem or a person who is viewed as a problem (Mountain).

is now acting as the adjective for Clover. Clover as the subject indicates a short period of good luck or some opportunity. Rider tells you this opportunity will be unfolding soon (as the Rider card can mean something will happen soon), or the period of good luck may occur while on a driving excursion since Rider can mean traveling, usually by car.

You can now see from the prior two examples that when it comes to Lenormand card combinations A + B does NOT EVER equal B + A. Always remember that the second card will always be acting as an adjective to the card that precedes it.

Taking the first two cards of the deck, you have Rider + Clover. The Rider is the subject of the card combination and represents a young man or someone who brings something to you—either a package or perhaps news. Clover is a short-lived opportunity, or a brief span of good luck. Combining these cards, what we have is the Rider brings you luck, something that increases your luck, or brings you news of a short-lived opportunity.

Reversing the card combination you now have Clover + Rider. Clover is now the subject card of this card combination and Rider

HOW TO READ LENORMAND CARDS

CHOOSING A SIGNIFICATOR CARD

Significators can be chosen ahead of time, or not, for any reading. This depends on whatever method you are accustomed to using. If you are new to card reading, then I do recommend, for your first few readings, to choose a significator card. When reading for a woman, you can use either the Goddess or Priestess card. When reading for a man, use either the God or Pharaoh card.

Significators can also be chosen based upon the area of life governed by that particular card as it pertains to the topic of your question. Here are a few examples for each card in the deck.

1. **RIDER:** a delivery person, or questions about deliveries and shipments

2. **CLOVER:** luck, new opportunities, gambling

3. **SHIP:** trips, shipping items in general, overseas or foreign matters

4. **HOUSE:** physical house, the home, family

5. **TREE:** health, doctor, family, ancestors

6. **CLOUDS:** worries, confusing issues

7. **SNAKE:** negative people or situations

8. **SARCOPHAGUS:** deceased loved ones, things that may come to an end, death

9. **FLOWERS:** gifts, engagements

10. **SICKLE:** separations, accidents, injuries

11. **CROOK & FLAIL:** Arguments, harsh words

12. **BIRDS:** verbal communication, older couple

13. **CHILD:** children, new endeavors

14. **DESERT FOX:** deceit, trickery, manipulation, intelligence, and for some, this card represents Work

15. **SACRED COW:** mother, mother-in-law, grandmother, windfall, general finances

16. **STARS:** hopes and wishes, creativity, esoteric matters

17. **IBIS:** relocation, changes

18. **DOG:** best friend, close friends, friendship, loyalty

19. **OBELISK:** authority figures, organizations, corporations

20. **GARDEN:** socializing, social network, celebrations, social gathering

21. **MOUNTAIN:** obstacles, enemies, delays

22. **CROSSROADS:** decisions, alternatives

23. **MICE:** Anxiety, fear, worry, loss, theft

24. **HEART:** love, romance, romantic relationships

25. **RING:** commitment, partnerships of all kinds, marriage

26. **SCROLL:** education, the occult, secrets, a teacher

27. **LETTER:** written communication of any kind

28. **GOD OR PHARAOH:** male

29. **GODDESS OR PRIESTESS:** female

30. **WATER LILY:** purity, harmony, sex

31. **SUN:** success, hopes

32. **MOON:** dreams, creativity, recognition, some use this as a card to represent Work

33. **KEY:** new opportunities, opening doors, successful outcome

34. **FISH:** money, prosperity

35. **ANCHOR:** stability, some use this as the Work card

36. **DJED PILLAR:** grief, extreme hardship, guilt

37. **CAT:** aloofness, distance (emotional or geographic), play

When choosing a significator, match it up as best you can to the subject of your question. For example, if you are asking about buying a house, choose the House card. If you're asking about finding a new job, use either the Desert Fox, Moon, or Anchor card (whichever you have decided upon to use as your Work card). When asking about a romantic relationship, use The Heart card, and so on.

You can either use the method that follows in determining placement of the significator in your reading, or you can choose all your cards for your reading at random and, if your pre-selected significator also appears, then that card position will carry extra weight in the reading.

There are 2 methods you can use in order to determine the significator for the topic of your question. If you are choosing a significator to represent a job, relationship, family, or some other issue, use one of the following methods. Decide for each reading before you start shuffling which method you will use. In my experience, both methods work equally well.

SIGNIFICATOR METHOD A

This method of choosing a significator card, and the manner in which it determines the choice of the other cards for a spread, has been published by Cortez (2002:171-174) in her discussion of her use of the 7-card "Lost Man Spread."

Lon Milo DuQuette (DuQuette 2005) later published this manner of choosing a significator and taught it to Rana George (R. George, pers. comm., 2013). It's obviously a very old method of cartomancy and we may never know where its true roots lay. Suffice it to say that it has been in use by many people over the decades, perhaps even over the centuries, when card reading first became popular in Europe back in the middle ages.

HOW TO READ LENORMAND CARDS

Based on the topic/subject of your question, decide ahead of time which card will represent the topic/subject of your reading. Look at that card, think of the topic/subject of your reading, and place the card randomly back into the deck.

Shuffle and concentrate on your question.

Cut the cards in whatever manner is your custom.

Turn the cards over and look for the pre-selected card. Once you find it, pull the 2 cards before it and the 2 cards that follow it. This forms a 5-card spread or any odd-numbered spread of your choosing. Just be sure an equal number of cards precedes and follows the significator card, which should always be exactly in the middle of the spread.

Should your pre-selected significator card be the last card of the deck so that it's on the bottom of the deck, it actually does have two cards following it. I have always viewed a stacked deck of cards as a continuous circle. The Order of the Golden Dawn also viewed the tarot deck as a continuous circuit with the sequence of the cards continuing on from the bottom card of the deck on back up to the top card of the deck (Mary K. Greer, pers. comm., 2013). Once you reach the bottom, go back to the card on top and the circle continues. Therefore, if your pre-selected significator card is on the bottom of the deck as you shuffled it, then the NEXT card in deck sequence will be the very top card of the deck. The second card from the top of the deck would then follow the card on the top, if you are choosing cards for a 5-card, or longer spread.

Your significator card can also appear on the very top of the deck as the very first or second card. Should your pre-selected card be the first card on top of the deck when you turn the deck over to look for it, technically it does have 2 previous cards. They are the two cards at the BOTTOM of the deck, so choose those. The first card of the spread will be the second-to-last card in the deck and the second card of your spread will be the last card in the deck.

This is the method I have always followed because it makes intrinsic sense to me, and in a Lenormand group on Facebook, Mary K. Greer (personal communication, 2013) pointed out to me that the method I proposed using was first used by the Golden Dawn magical association in the early 1900s for Tarot readings.

SIGNIFICATOR METHOD B

Decide which card shall signify the topic of your reading.

Shuffle while concentrating on your question.

Cut the deck.

Then draw the cards from the top of the deck for your reading. Using this method, the pre-selected significator card remains in the deck. It may appear in the spread, or it may not. All cards for the spread are chosen at random from the top of the deck. Should your pre-chosen significator appear in the spread, this card position carries extra importance.

86

THE 3-CARD SPREAD

The 3-Card Spread gives a brief overview of a situation or a quick answer to a simple question. You may use either method for choosing a significator, then lay the cards out moving left to right:

CARD 1 + CARD 2 + CARD 3

Card 1 will be the Subject card. This card represents the main topic of your reading.

Card 2 works as an Adjective here. It will give you further details about Card 1 and or Card 2.

Card 3 also works as an Adjective. It will provide additional details about Card 1 or Card 2.

To sum up the reading, you then read the card combination of Card 1 + Card 3.

You can then read all cards together as though they create a single sentence in order to determine what you may expect.

For example, I had a client come to me asking about a neighbor who was making all sorts of noise in the apartment above hers. The landlord would not do anything about it and even told her that if she didn't like it, she could just break her lease and move. This

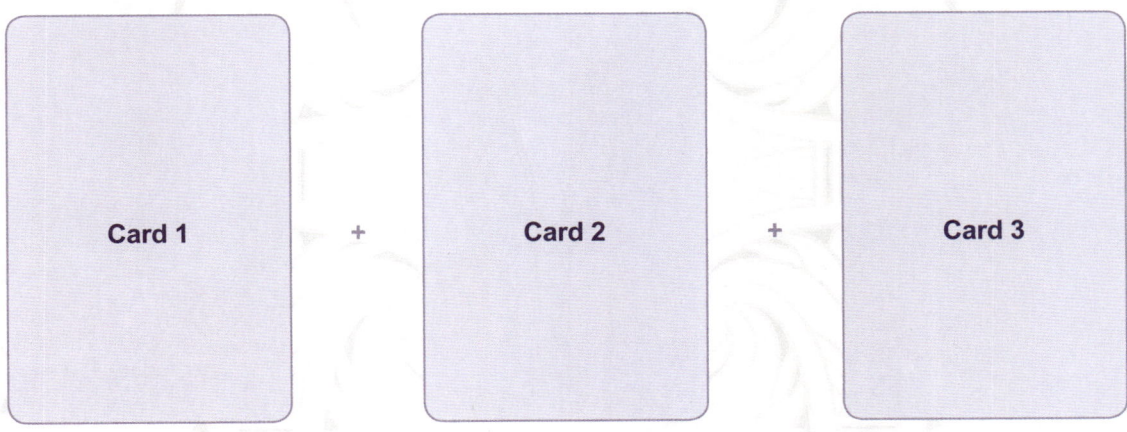

HOW TO READ LENORMAND CARDS

would mean she would be in default of her lease and would have to pay her landlord extra money to get out of the apartment. She was losing sleep and was at a loss as to what she could do. She asked of the cards:

"What can I do about my noisy neighbor?"

I drew three cards for her:

The **Letter** serves as the subject or topic of the reading. In this case, that told me we were dealing with a written document. Given the nature of her question, I took Letter to represent her lease with the landlord.

When I see **Tree** in a reading, I always automatically think health or perhaps extended family. This meaning did not seem to fit the subject matter of her question.

Dog represents loyalty and friendship, a guide, or helper of some sort. I took this to mean someone could help her with this situation and since she had already talked to the noisy neighbor, who was quite rude to her, I could discount him as the "help" she was to receive.

After pondering her reading a few minutes it dawned on me that Andy Boroveshengra (2014) identifies the Dog card with sometimes representing

Letter + **Tree** + **Dog**

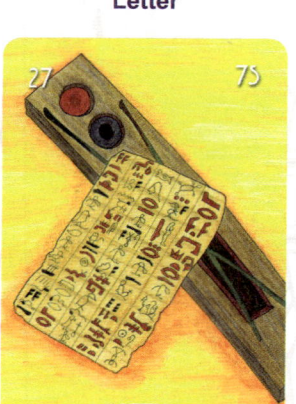

a health care professional. Based upon the presence of the Tree card, that interpretation made sense.

Letter represented her lease. Tree indicated there was a clause in her lease pertaining to health. Reading Tree as representing health, this then indicated that the Dog represented a doctor, and looking at all three cards to sum things up for her, combining Letter + Dog I told her that she needed to read over her lease carefully because there was a clause about health issues, and that perhaps that was how she could get out of her lease and move, since the poor woman was not getting any sleep due to all the noise. I suggested she could perhaps get her doctor to write the landlord a note.

She later contacted me to say that yes, there was a clause that if a tenant had a severe health condition that required them to move and they could prove this with a doctor's note, they would be released from their lease without any further consequences. She then went to see her doctor and after explaining the situation to her, she wrote my client a letter. My client then provided the letter to the landlord who then, according to the health clause of his own lease, had to release her from her commitment, so my client was able to relocate.

For any reading, if a card appears to be leading somewhere, or you wish for further details about it, draw 1–3 cards from the deck. I shuffle the card pile three times while focusing on whichever card I need more details about. I then at random draw 1, 2, or 3 more cards. Then I lay them in a column underneath the card they are discussing.

A 5-CARD SPREAD

The 5-Card Spread will provide more details than the 3-Card Spread. It consists of the use of five cards arranged in a single line that are read from left to right like a sentence.

How to Read Lenormand Cards

A simple Lenormand reading consists of an odd number of cards: therefore, 3, 5, 7, 9, 11, and so on. Regardless of the method used, the card in the center will most likely represent the topic of your question or will be somehow directly related to the topic, whether it was pre-selected as the subject or significator card or not. This is the pivotal card around which all other cards rotate.

The way I read a line spread of cards is very simple. I see the cards as representing a progression through a brief period of time (usually 1–8 weeks) from past to future moving from left to right. For a 5-Card Spread, the reading order would be as follows:

CARDS 1 AND 2: The Past

CARDS 2 AND 3: Represent something in the past that needs to be released or may have been holding you back in the situation

CARD 3: The Present

CARDS 3 AND 4: Represent something you either can do or may need to do in order to help things to work out favorably for you. This card combination often offers advice in general that may

1 + 2 + 3 + 4 + 5.

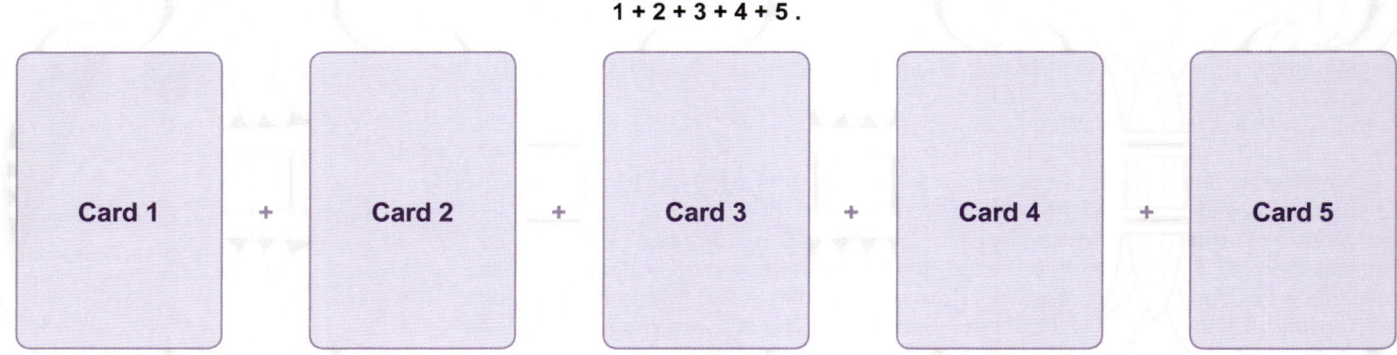

or may not be directly related to the subject of your question.

CARDS 4 AND 5: The Future

A more thorough method is to read the spread in paired card combinations. To read a spread consisting of five cards, for example, in this manner you do the following:

1 2 3 4 5

Read cards 1 and 2 together as a pair, keeping in mind Lenormand syntax. The second card will always serve as an adjective to the first card, giving you more information about the first card. Cards 1 and 2 represent the past.

Next, **read cards 2 and 3 as a pair**, keeping syntactical rules in mind. This will be the immediate passing influence. Card 2 is the subject while Card 3 is the adjective.

Read cards 3 and 4 as a pair. This represents the present or the very near future. In this case, Card 3 is the subject and Card 4 is the adjective.

Cards 4 and 5 read as a pair represents how things are most likely to develop in the situation. Card 4 is now the subject of this particular card combination and Card 5 serves as the adjective.

Finally, **go back to read cards 1 and 5 as a pair**. This will give you a summary of the situation or supply some information that may be about something unexpected. Keep in mind Card 1 will represent the subject while Card 5 will act as an adjective providing additional details about Card 1.

How to Read Lenormand Cards

A Sample 5-Card Reading

A client came to me asking about her career focus. Her question was:

What would be a good career choice or direction for me?

I chose the Priestess as my client's significator card, since she is female. I then shuffled while concentrating on her question. Upon cutting the deck, I looked for her significator and its placement within the deck that then determined the first two and final two cards of the spread.

My client received the following cards:

Garden + **Tree** + **Priestess** +

The Garden represents socializing. It often indicates getting out and being around people. So this immediately tells me that, for her job, she considers it very important to have a job that encourages interaction with others. She enjoys being around people and finds work much more enjoyable when she can make a few friends in the workplace.

The Garden can represent a gathering of people and it can also symbolize dealing with the public in general. For gatherings, this can be anything from a family bbq in the backyard to a rock concert where there are thousands of people who don't know each other. The Garden is all about getting out among people. It can even represent a physical garden as well, or flowers and plants.

Next, my client received the Tree. Tree is the card of health, longevity, stability, and deep roots. The Tree tells me that she considers it important that a job make her feel secure regarding her income, which is an opinion most people share. She has ideas of what she would like to do for a career, but she is worried that such jobs won't afford her many benefits and she would not want her entire paycheck going toward a health crisis should one ever occur (hopefully not!). Tree also represents her desire for steady, dependable work and to work with others (combined with the Garden) who are reliable co-workers. This indicates that she is a conscientious person and does not wish to be left holding the bag if others are not living up to expectations in the workplace. I feel this may have happened to her in the past—and more than once. She desires co-workers to be as reliable and conscientious as she is.

Key + **Child**

93

HOW TO READ LENORMAND CARDS

Tree can also denote Nature and being out among plants.

Now, what's fascinating here is that the Garden can, for a career, represent a gardener or a florist. Combined with Tree it is fairly obvious. This first card combination is already pointing in a very specific direction for my client. The Garden and Tree are telling me that working with plants would be a good direction for her. Now, this could be in a plant nursery, a florist's shop, or even on a flower farm. My client lives in Miami, so there are bound to be a lot of places that grow plants for sale, not to mention the Florida Everglades, so that's another option regarding that line of work.

If she does not feel she would be happy with gardening or floristry, then this card combination of Garden + Tree is indicating that she needs a job that deals with the outdoors or Nature in some way. Perhaps a conservationist or working with a company that deals with conserving nature or working in a forest preserve or something along those lines. This may have something to do with the Florida beaches is yet another option. The preserving of endangered species would be yet another idea.

The next card, the Priestess, is my client's significator. As such, it is first combined with Tree to form the card combination of Tree + Priestess. I am definitely seeing Tree as representing Nature now, so this card combination tells me that Nature is very important to my client.

Then, I examine Priestess + Key for the next card combination. Here, Key provides further information about the Priestess card, which represents my client. Key is saying that it's important to her to be successful in whatever career path she eventually chooses.

The fourth card is The Key and here it represents success. Keys unlock doors, so the Key card can represent a new opportunity coming her way. Many people consider old keys to be lucky charms, so this card can also represent a turn toward better luck. This is in her near future since The Key follows her significator. She can expect better things coming up soon for her.

The Child concludes her reading. It represents new things (also children). Usually, this card appears to represent a new endeavor or a change of direction. What The Child card tells me is that my client has grown bored with what she currently does for a living. She would like to try something new and move in a completely new direction, but she is unsure of what she would like to try to focus on, so she may be feeling kind of stuck.

With Key preceding it, Key + Child is telling her that her true success lies with being nurturing toward something. It may have to do with childcare, but I really don't get anything about taking care of children from this reading. I think it has more to do with nurturing something else, perhaps like the environment in general or perhaps working with a particular endangered species or an endangered natural habitat. The environment and animals need our care, so, in the Lenormand, they can come up as a child in need of love and nurturing. It's definitely something to do with some aspect of Nature, so, at this point, I recommend my client have a good think about it and see if anything specific comes to mind. The Key right after her significator promises long-term success with this new career, also, and The Child card is saying she will enjoy it so much that her work will always seem new and exciting.

A few days later, my client provided some feedback on her reading. She told me she has always loved Nature and would love to become involved in some conservatory work for the environment or endangered species. She also lives close to the Florida Everglades, so that is a definite possibility she is seriously considering.

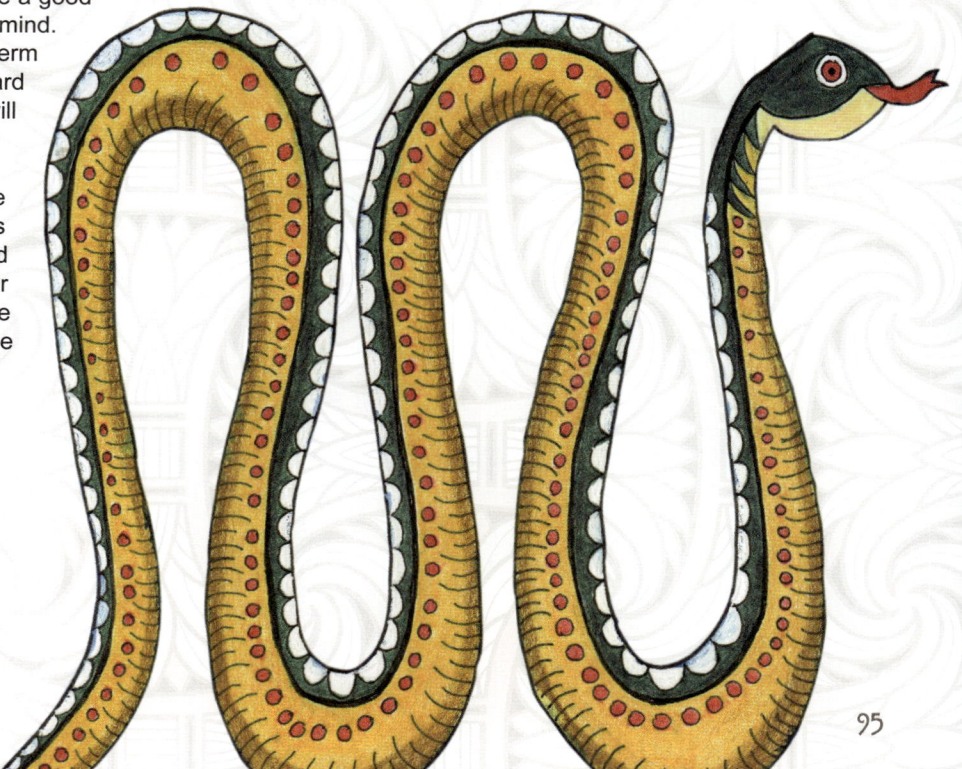

How to Read Lenormand Cards

7+-Card Spreads

Longer line spreads are read in the same manner as a five-card spread, except the number of cards chosen will differ. The significator card will always be the central card so an equal number of cards must be chosen before and following the significator.

An example of a 9-Card Spread where the fifth card is the significator would be:

1 + 2 + 3 + 4 + 5 + 6 + 7 + 8 + 9.

You would then read the combinations, which would line up as:

1 AND 2: the distant past

2 AND 3: the immediate past (2 – 4 weeks)

3 AND 4: a passing influence

4 AND 5: the present

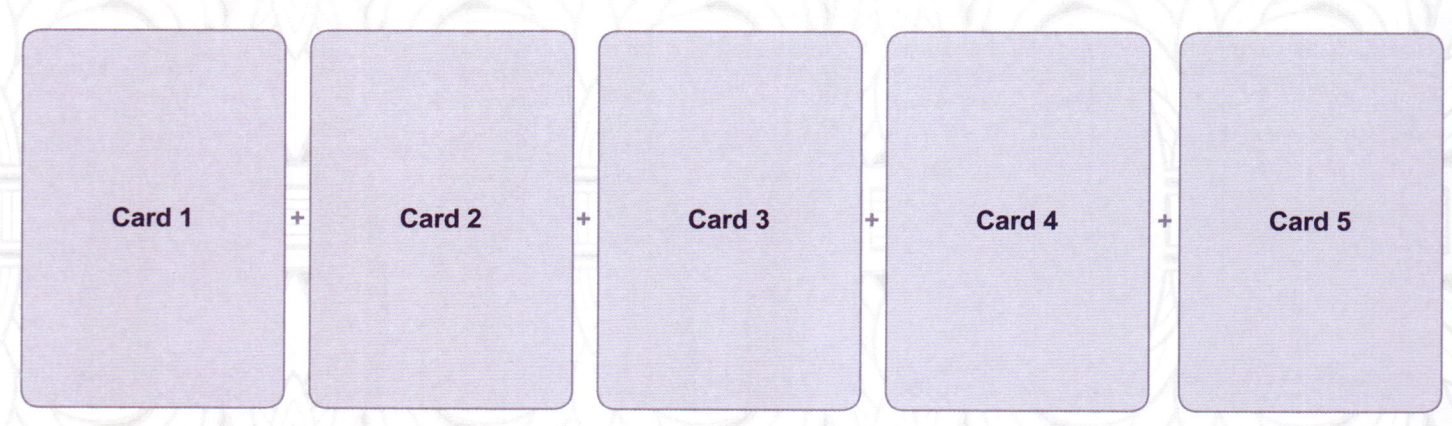

5 AND 6: a new influence

6 AND 7: near future (next 2 – 4 weeks)

7 AND 8: distant future

8 AND 9: general outcome

Then, you can sum up by reading the card combo of **1 and 9**.

The same method applies for a spread consisting of 7, 11, 13, or any other odd number of cards.

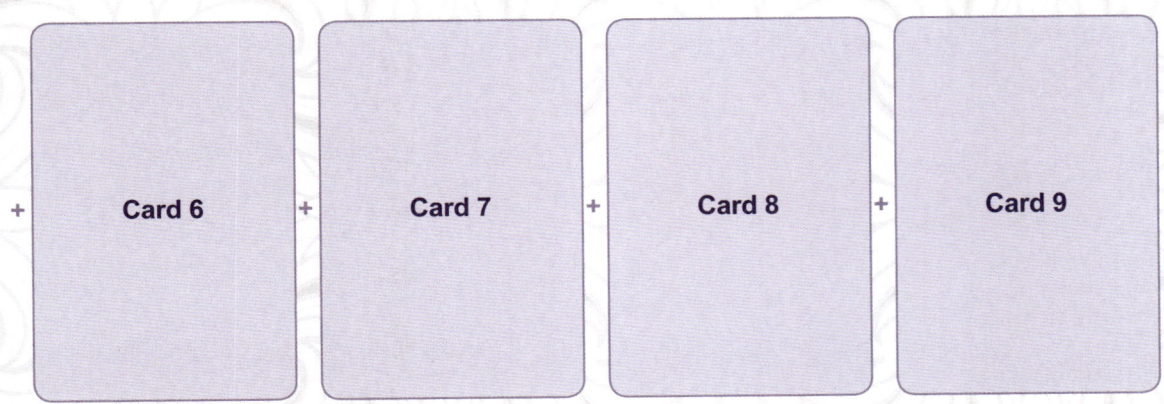

HOW TO READ LENORMAND CARDS

THE 10-CARD PYRAMID OF ISIS SPREAD

The pyramid-shape is very commonly used in Tarot readings, however, I have not seen it (to my knowledge) used for Lenormand. That is most likely about to change, as there are a number of books very soon to be published on Lenormand making it much more accessible to the public at large.

This is an adaptation of a pyramid spread I have been using with Tarot clients for over twenty years, applicable for use with Lenormand cards.

You will be using a total of 10 cards laid out in this manner:

Cards are laid out in the order shown and each row is first read from left to right. No significator card is used for this spread.

CARDS 1–4: The foundation or contributing factors to the situation under question

CARDS 5–7: Things you need to work on, or obstacles facing you

CARDS 8 AND 9: Helpful allies, things working in your favor

CARD 10: Most probable outcome

Another way to use this spread is as follows:

CARDS 1–4: Distant past

CARDS 5–7: Present

CARDS 8–9: Advice

CARD 10: Most probable outcome

Make your choice ahead of time as to which version of the Pyramid of Isis Spread you wish to use. Shuffle the cards as you are accustomed and lay them out, cards 1 – 10.

READING ROWS

The rows are meant to be read in pairs and then in larger combinations. For example:

Row 1 is to be read as: cards 1 and 2 read as pair, then cards 2 and 3, and finally cards 3 and 4 read as a pair. Finally, read cards 1–4 as a 4-card combination. In other words, create a story using those four cards.

Move on up to **Row 2** and focus on cards 5 and 6 as a pair, then cards 6 and 7 as a pair. Read all three as a 3-card combination.

Next, read **Row 3** as a pair, cards 8 and 9.

Row 4 card 10 is read in isolation as the most likely outcome to the situation under question.

For additional details, go back to Card 1 and read it as the adjective giving further information about Card 10.

For still further details, you can now go back over the spread and read it in the following manner:

Examine cards 1 and 4 as a pair. These two cards tell you what you bring to the present from your past. These usually sum up personal traits of you or the person for whom you are reading.

Next, examine cards 5 and 7. These two cards will tell you what type of an attitude you or your client brings to the situation, for good or ill.

Finally, read cards 8 and 10. These two cards will tell you the chances your desired outcome has of manifesting. If you have no vested interest in the outcome, then you may choose to disregard this card combination.

HOW TO READ LENORMAND CARDS

READING PYRAMID SIDES

Regardless of the method you use for the Pyramid of Isis Spread, in order to gain even more information, you may choose to read the Lenormand cards moving up along either side of the Pyramid of Isis.

First you read the left-hand side, then the right-hand side.

Reading cards 1, 5, 8, and 10 from the left-hand side represent what other people involved in the situation contribute for good or ill.

Reading cards 4, 7, 9 and 10 along the right-hand side of the Pyramid of Isis represent unknown or unrecognized influences on the situation under question. These cards are to be read in pairs first, so cards 1 and 5 followed by cards 8 and 10. For a nice summary of what others are contributing to the situation you can then also read cards 1 and 10. For the unknown influences read cards 4 and 7 as a pair, then cards 9 and 10 as a pair. Finally sum them up by reading cards 4 and 10 as a pair.

READING A SUMMARY

Lastly, for an overall summary of the reading you may also choose to read cards 6 and 10 as a pair.

SAMPLE PYRAMID OF ISIS SPREAD

My friend Jessica's question was:

What sort of advice or guidance can the cards provide regarding her spiritual development.

Birds + **Mice**

Firstly, I examine cards 1 – 4 that represent the foundation or factors contributing to the situation.

Cards 1–4 are Birds + Mice + Tree + Crossroads

Birds represents communication and, since Jessica's question revolves around her spirituality, when we relate the Birds card to her question, it implies some form of spiritual communication. Mice represents fears and worries here. In my line of work, I have run across countless people who wish to communicate with their spirit guides or develop their intuitive abilities, but they are fearful of the entire process and of what they might learn. Their fear can act as a major stumbling block and this is what Mice is representing about Jessica. She yearns for deeper communication with her spirit guides, but Mice, representing her fear, stands in her way.

How to Read Lenormand Cards

Tree + **Crossroads**

Tree, when related to Jessica's question, represents lineage and ancestry. It is suggesting that the type of spirit helpers around Jessica at this time are either deceased loved ones or family members from further back in her lineage whom she may have never met. Pairing Mice + Tree indicates that Jessica's own sense of stability will help her to overcome her fears. Crossroads concludes Row 1 and represents choices and being faced with alternatives. The choice here would be for Jessica to either continue on her spiritual quest and focus on communicating with her deceased loved ones and/or ancestors or to give in to her fears. Considering that Tree is a card of firm foundation, I feel that Jessica will chose to investigate further because she is very interested in establishing some form of spiritual communication. Therefore, I see her getting past her initial fears and insecurities about the process.

Row 2 consists of cards 5–7 that represent things Jessica needs to work on or possible obstacles she may face. Jessica received House + Heart + Mountain.

House represents Jessica's home, and Heart is simply saying that "home is where the heart is," meaning that Jessica feels very secure in her home; she enjoys it and views it as her safe haven. Given her underlying fears, represented by the Mice, she may be fearful that the process of spirit communication may allow some negative forces into her home. In order to avoid that, she will need to take the necessary precautions before every attempt at spirit communication, and this is easily accomplished by calling upon spiritual protection or imagining herself surrounded by protective white light.

Mountain is problematic. Following Heart, Mountain can simply be saying that although Jessica is very interested in embarking upon a more spiritual lifestyle and discovering what her true spiritual gifts are, there may be a major stumbling block concerning how she feels about the situation, with Heart representing her feelings about it. Note that, in the spread, Heart is directly above Mice and Tree, with Mice representing Jessica's fears. Once again, I see her fears holding her back; however, with the safety and love of her home represented here, Mountain acts more as a delay than a direct block to her spiritual ambitions. I believe that once Jessica gets past her fear, then there will be nothing to hold her back.

House   +   **Heart**   +   **Mountain**

 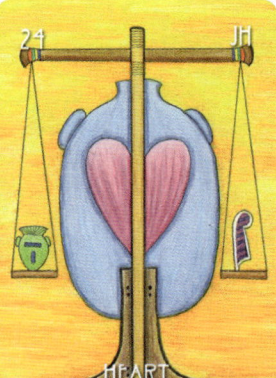 

How to Read Lenormand Cards

Rider + **Sarcophagus**

Cards 8 and 9 represent helpful allies or things working in Jessica's favor. Here she received Rider and Sarcophagus. Rider represents someone bringing something to her, or perhaps this is a young man from Jessica's own lineage who is around her at this time wishing to act as a spirit guide for her. Sarcophagus follows, and although traditionally a card of endings, given the subject matter of Jessica's question and the fact that spirit communication is the topic of discussion, I see the Sarcophagus as representing a deceased individual. As the adjective to the Rider card, Sarcophagus is telling me that the Rider either brings to Jessica someone who is deceased or the Rider represents a deceased individual. This card combination tells us that Jessica's helpful ally in this matter is clearly someone in spirit form.

Moon

Card 10 represents the most probably outcome for Jessica and here she has received The Moon. The Moon represents recognition and honors, so this tells me that despite her fears, represented by Mice, acting as a possible major stumbling block for her as represented by Mountain, Jessica will succeed in her spiritual quest. At some point, she will do very well in her quest to develop her spirituality and any latent spiritual gifts she may have.

This information represents the general overview of the reading. Now it's time to dig deeper in order to gain further information about Jessica's spiritual development and what she can expect.

How to Read Lenormand Cards

| Birds | + | Crossroads |

The next card pair I examine consists of cards 1 and 4. These two cards represent what Jessica is bringing forward from her past and how it is influencing the current situation. The cards she received are Birds and Crossroads.

The Birds card represents her skills at communicating with others. Jessica works in the healthcare profession, so she deals with patients and their families on a regular basis. Crossroads represents choices and, following Birds, it is saying that the method by which Jessica decides to communicate with her spirit guides is strictly up to her, but she will have to decide on a particular method.

House   +   **Mountain**

Next, I examine cards 5 and 7 that tell Jessica what sort of an attitude she brings to her spiritual endeavors. Jessica received House + Mountain. The House represents Jessica's home, while Mountain indicates there is some type of issue in the home that may impact upon her spiritual endeavors. Note that Sarcophagus is directly above Mountain. When you begin to work with larger spreads, it is important to examine all surrounding cards. Sarcophagus has already been interpreted as meaning the departed, or spirits. Seeing that card directly above Mountain makes me wonder if there is already a spirit in Jessica's home who may attempt to interfere with her spiritual development.

How to Read Lenormand Cards

Rider + **Moon**

Cards 8 and 10 are read next and they represent the chances your desired outcome has actually manifesting into reality. Jessica received Rider and Moon. Rider represents messages or news coming to Jessica and Moon tells her what form the messages or news will take. The Moon can represent dreams and, based upon that, I deduce that the form the messages will take will be those that occur within dreams. I would then instruct Jessica to pay close attention to her dreams and perhaps keep a dream journal.

Next, we examine what other people may contribute to the situation by looking at cards 1, 5, 8, and 10 along the left-hand side of the Pyramid of Isis Spread. The cards Jessica received here are: Birds + House + Rider + Moon.

Birds represents communication, here of a spiritual nature if we relate the card back to Jessica's question. House indicates such communication will occur in her home, which makes perfect sense, since this is not the type of thing a person can do in public. Rider represents messages, and following House indicates messages will be received at home. Moon concludes this portion of Jessica's reading and here represents dreams, further indicating messages will come to Jessica in her dreams. Considering the spiritual nature of the information in this portion of the reading, I can only surmise that the others involved in the situation are Jessica's own spirit guides who will help her through the process of her further spiritual development. This is verified when I examine cards 1 and 10 to sum up these four cards. The card combination of Birds + Moon indicates communication of a dream-like, or perhaps spiritual nature.

How to Read Lenormand Cards

Next, I examine the cards along the right-hand side of the Pyramid of Isis Spread so I look at cards 4, 7, 9, and 10. The cards along the right-hand side represent unknown or unrecognized influences upon the situation. These cards are: Crossroads + Mountain + Sarcophagus + Moon. Note that Moon is included in both of these card combinations as the outcome card, but that the card that precedes it is different in each case, thus resulting in a different card combination.

Crossroads indicates Jessica's choice to move past her fears and embark further upon her spiritual studies, or to allow her fears to dictate her behavior. Mountain indicates delays or possible obstacles. Paired with Crossroads, the Mountain card is indicating Jessica maybe overwhelmed by choices just generally speaking. She may not like to have too many alternatives to choose from and feels more comfortable when the way ahead is clear.

Sarcophagus represents the spirit world and spirits in general, if we relate it directly to Jessica's question. Paired with Mountain, Sarcophagus is indicating there maybe

Crossroads + **Mountain** + **Sarcophagus** + **Moon**

delays regarding Jessica's further spiritual development, but they won't be a result of Jessica's fears. These possible delays will result from Jessica's own spirit guides and helpers deciding when it will be best for them to start communicating with Jessica. In other words, they wish for her to be ready for such communication. They may not feel that Jessica is quite ready yet.

Sarcophagus + Moon indicates once again, that it will be in dreams that Jessica will be able to communicate with her spirit allies. Spirit guides and angels often communicate with us in our dreams because when in the dream state our natural defenses are down and we are fully relaxed, thus it is easier for them to reach us to impart messages and guidance.

To sum up this section, we then look at cards 4 and 10 as a pair, which are Crossroads and Moon. Once again, the cards tell us that Jessica is faced with alternatives and choices, but Moon indicates she will recognize what her choices are and may arrive at a creative manner through which she can communicate with her spirit guides that is non-threatening to her, thus helping her to overcome her fears represented by the Mice card and go on toward being successful in her spiritual endeavor.

Finally, to summarize the entire reading, I examine cards 6 and 10, which are Heart and Moon. Heart indicates that Jessica's heart is in the right place. She is very much interested in advancing her own spiritual development and can be a very dedicated student. Moon indicates that her own creativity will lead to success in her spiritual endeavors that eventually may even lead to her receiving some sort of recognition or fame should she decide to apply her spiritual communication skills toward helping others.

Heart + **Moon**

HOW TO READ LENORMAND CARDS

THE QUINTESSENCE OF A READING

A Lenormand reading can be summed up in two ways: as shown prior, you can simply read the first and last cards of the spread as a two-card combination. This can often provide a nice overview of the reading.

The second method is called the quintessence. There are two methods for arriving at the quintessence.

THE FIRST METHOD consists of adding up the numbers on the playing cards associated with each card. The shorthand names of the playing cards are noted on the upper right-hand corner of each card:

D = Diamonds

C = Clubs

S = Spades

H = Hearts

J = Jack

Q = Queen

K = King

A = Ace

So, for example, the KH noted in the upper right-hand corner of the House card would denote the King of Hearts as being the playing card associated with the House card. When adding up the playing card numbers to arrive at the quintessence:

Jacks are 11

Queens are 12

Kings are 13

Aces are 1

THE SECOND METHOD consists of adding the number on the cards together; as in:

4 House + 9 Flowers + 3 Ship = 4 + 9 + 3 = 16

The quintessence would be 16, which represents The Stars card.

Now, should your reading consist of higher cards, for instance: 30 Water Lily + 21 Mountain + 37 Cat, you will receive a much higher sum than the highest numbered card in the deck. In this case you would arrive at: 30 + 21 + 37 = 88. What you would then need to do is add the two digits of the number together to arrive at the quintessence: 88 = 8 + 8 = 16, which again, would be The Stars card as the quintessence of the reading.

Decide ahead of time which method you will use and make it your own. Use the same method every time you arrive at a quintessence. Do not switch back and forth between methods. It's fine to experiment a few times in the beginning, but once you figure out which is your preferred method, stick to it. The quintessence can give you a nice little forecast to make based upon the reading itself or it can provide additional information. In some cases it may appear to make no sense at first, as in the example that follows.

The students of my online Lenormand class were attempting to identify the gender of a grandchild one of the student's sons was expecting. It was very early on in his wife's pregnancy. In situations where you are trying to figure out the gender of a baby, this is the time when the playing card association of the Lenormand cards can be very important. If one or more of the cards drawn are associated with a court card, that would identify the gender of the baby regardless of what the actual cards mean. The God and Pharaoh cards would represent a boy while the Goddess and Priestess cards would represent a girl.

However, readings don't always cooperate and sometimes you may not have any court cards appear in a spread; so then what do you do if the question involves gender?

That's when the Quintessence can be of great importance. The Quintessence provides you with the essential overall message the reading is trying to convey to you. Therefore, the Quintessence card sums up the reading.

So, looking at a reading Susan posted asking about the gender of her son's baby, she drew:

14 Desert Fox + 27 Letter + 25 Ring

Add them together and you get 66. Since it is larger than 37 this card must be further reduced by adding 6 + 6, which gives us 12. Twelve is the Quintessence of this reading. That gives us The Birds card.

= 12 Birds

Looking at The Birds, we see that its playing card association is the 7 of Diamonds. Unfortunately, this method didn't give us a gender; however, Birds is a timing card, meaning "in 2." I interpreted this for the class as meaning the couple will discover the gender of their baby within 2 weeks or 2 months from the time of the reading. As it worked out, Susan's daughter-in-law had an ultra sound done two weeks later that revealed the gender of the baby, just as the Birds card had predicted.

In conclusion, this serves as a good example of when the quintessence does not appear to make any sense; make note of it anyway because it may be indicating something closely related to the subject of your question or providing additional information that will become clear in a short while.

There are many types of spreads you can use with the Lenormand cards. For a thorough discussion of the Grand Tableau, which uses 36 cards, I refer you to Boroveshengra (2014) listed in the References Cited section.

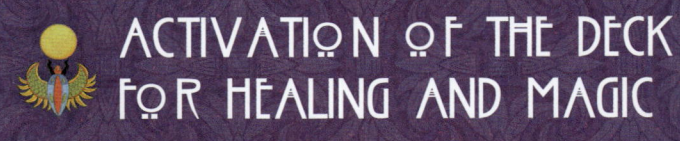

ACTIVATION OF THE DECK FOR HEALING AND MAGIC

INTRODUCTION

The Lenormand system is a method of divination only. A typical Lenormand deck is not meant to be used for anything other than forecasting the future, giving advice, and for guidance. However, when I began receiving channeled messages from the gods in the form of these card images, I was also told that The Egyptian Lenormand would contain real energies that could later be unlocked by anyone using the deck, provided they had the key. This chapter serves as that key.

As you will have seen when you first looked through the cards, there are two extra cards for which the front and backs are identical. These two cards are referred to as "The Activation Keys."

    The design on the card back is the Eye of Horus, known as the Wadjet. According to Egyptian mythology, Horus, the son of the gods Isis and Osiris, engaged in a battle with his uncle, Set. Set had been brother to both Isis and Osiris, but he coveted the throne of Osiris, so he murdered his brother. Set then attempted to kill Horus once he had been born, but failed. When Horus came of age to claim his father's throne, he was required to defeat Set in order to regain the throne from his uncle.

Activation of the Deck for Healing and Magic

During the battle, Set pierces one of the eyes of Horus, which Horus loses as a result. The god Thoth is said to have restored the eye by placing the moon or the sun into the empty socket (it varies, depending on the version of the myth one reads). This then became the Eye of Horus, a very powerful amulet that is still used by many today.

The Eye of Horus is said to represent protection, healing, strength, and courage. The Eye of Horus has been used in the form of an amulet since the time of ancient Egypt and today you can find it as jewelry. Worn with the intention of being an amulet, the Eye of Horus becomes much more than some cool symbol from ancient Egypt. It becomes a container of real power and can actually send out the energies of protection, healing, strength, and courage to the one who wears it.

I channeled the image of the card back from the gods, just as I had channeled all the other images for the deck. When the gods gave me the image for the card back I was told:

"This is the Key."

That did confuse me, since the Lenormand does contain a Key card that is a traditional part of the Lenormand system. I asked my guides what they meant by the Eye of Horus being the Key, and I received the following explanation:

The Wadjet is an opener of the way for these images. All images contain energies that remain dormant until they are activated by the Wadjet, which then therefore serves as the Key. Once used in this manner and with this intention, the Wadjet will activate the energies contained in all images included in this system. The images will become alive with energy that the user will then be able to channel according to their intention.

In short, what you hold in your hands is not merely a deck of divination. *The Egyptian Lenormand*, when used with the proper intention and focus, also becomes a tool of healing and of magic.

How to Activate Your Deck

Your deck does not arrive activated for healing or magical use. You must do this yourself as the user so you can imbue the deck with your own unique energy. This is a very simple and quick process. All you need is the following. Gather:

- The two Activation Keys, or Eye of Horus cards

- The Key card

- A white candle

- Safe holder for the candle

- A lighter

- The remainder of the deck in numerical order

Personally, I do not recommend the use of matches when lighting candles or incense for spiritual work. Matches are made from sulfur and, in my own line of work, I have noticed many times a negative entity will announce its presence with the smell of sulfur. Hence, I do not use matches. I use a lighter.

Be sure the holder you choose for your candle fits it. This means a votive should go into a votive holder, a taper should go into a taper holder, and so on. Please be sure the candle is located in a safe area away from curtains or papers that may catch on fire should a stray spark land on them. You will need to allow the candle to burn itself out in a safe place, so also be sure pets (or children) are kept away from the candle. Most animals are afraid of fire, that's true, but I have often heard of curious cats who get too close to a candle flame and knock the candle over. Please take the necessary precautions whenever you are using candles.

Be sure you lay your items down on a clean and uncluttered surface. Lay the first Eye of Horus Activation card down, The Key card in the center, followed by the second

Eye of Horus   **The Key**   **Eye of Horus**

Deck

ACTIVATION OF THE DECK FOR HEALING AND MAGIC

Eye of Horus Activation card on the right. You should now have a row of three cards in front of you. Place the deck in front of the row of three cards. The deck should be resting in the center between you and the cards. Place the candle holder behind the row of three cards in the center, so the candle should be behind The Key card.

CLEANSING YOUR CANDLE

I always recommend cleansing and charging a candle before ritual or magical use. Candles, as with any item, can pick up energies from their manufacturer, during shipping, and also while being stored on a store shelf. If you are going to use them for ritual or magical work, it is always best to cleanse them first.

You cleanse a candle simply by holding it and rubbing outward from the center to both ends. Be sure to also include the wick. You can then visualize gray or black smoke leaving the candle from both ends, as it becomes purified from any undesired energies it may have picked up along its way to your home. Many times, I have felt a candle actually grow lighter in my hands, as though it has lost a bit of weight. This always tells me that where the candle came from had some negative energy.

I recommend cleansing your candle for about 10-20 seconds. This process does not take long at all. Once cleansed, you can now charge your candle for your intention.

CHARGING YOUR CANDLE

Charging is the opposite of cleansing. The cleansing process is to clear the candle of other energies, while the charging process is meant to place energy into the candle—specifically your own unique energy and the energy of your intention, or what you desire to manifest as a result of the use of this candle.

In the case of activating your deck, again, grab the candle from the center and now rub inward toward the center from both ends. Remember to include the wick and imagine your energy and intention moving along the wick, down to the base of the candle. The intention you need to hold in your mind or repeat aloud is:

> I place my energy into this candle for the express purpose of activating my copy of *The Egyptian Lenormand* for use in healing and magic.

The length of time the charging process requires varies from individual to individual and is based on how well you can focus on a single intention without allowing other thoughts to interfere. Usually, it's a 30-second process, but for some, it may be longer if you allow other thoughts to enter your mind. Should other thoughts occur to you, simply bring your focus back to your candle and your intention until the candle feels "right" to you.

Some signs that your candle has been properly charged include a feeling of added weight, tingling, or heat. Also, bear in mind the more you rub the candle, the hotter it will become due to your own body heat. That's normal, but sometimes the heat level can be much warmer than what can be explained as the mere transference of body heat.

Once your candle is charged, you may then place it in its holder. Now you're ready to perform some magic.

PERFORMING MAGIC

You will be addressing the Egyptian deities from whom I channeled this deck. However, if you are not comfortable with that idea, you can focus on calling in the White Light, or your own angels and spirit guides. Just reword the invocation differently—that's all that is required.

Light the candle and repeat the following four times (the number 4 being sacred to the ancient Egyptians as the number of divine order) while keeping a hand on each of the Activation Cards, palms down, covering the image:

*Until now these cards have been
Merely images printed on paper.
Today mighty Isis, wise Thoth,
Protective Anubis, and powerful Amun-Ra
All breathe Life into these cards
Blessing them with the ability
To channel both energies
Of healing and of magic.
Isis, Thoth, Anubis, and Amun-Ra,
I ask each of You to place these energies
Into this deck.
I thank You for Your Presence here today
And for the unique blessings You have bestowed upon these cards.
May these cards always serve my highest good
And the highest good of all concerned.
Em Hotep.*

Repeat four times aloud or to yourself while keeping your hands, palm down, over each image of the Eye of Horus. "Em Hotep" is Egyptian for, "In peace," and is a respectful manner in which to say good-bye to the gods after uttering a prayer.

Once you have repeated the invocation four times The Key card in the center is now charged. Divide the deck into two equal halves, placing The Key card in the center of the deck. It should be placed between The Obelisk (card number 19) and The Garden (card number 20).

Reassemble the deck.

Holding the intention of activating the deck for both healing and magical use, shuffle the deck carefully seven times. Place the deck back on your work surface.

Allow the candle to burn completely out. When it has gone out, you may bury any candle remains on your property, or if you rent, within a potted plant.

Keep your deck in a safe place.

Your deck is now fully activated to not only serve as a divinatory Lenormand deck of cards, but it also contains energies that can aid in healing and magic as well. Should you ever find your deck seems to be losing its charge or perhaps it has come into contact

ACTIVATION OF THE DECK FOR HEALING AND MAGIC

with a very upset person who has left their energy on the cards, feel free to repeat the activation ceremony.

Please save the two Activation cards, the double-sided Eye of Horus cards, in case you ever feel the need to reactivate your deck. You will also need both cards for channeling healing energy and magical use.

REACTIONS OF MY STUDENTS UPON COMPLETING THE DECK ACTIVATION CEREMONY

My online students learned how to do basic readings with the cards before I took the class through the Activation Ceremony. They were already accustomed to using the cards strictly for divinatory purposes. Once they performed the Activation Ceremony for their particular deck, they began to notice that it felt different. Their experiences are noted below and shared with their kind permission.

I feel that I am one with my deck, as if there is a deity with them, one that will help with each reading.

~ Bernadette Hyde Krause

I did feel an energy in the cards; it was undeniable and also I know/feel that they are truly mine, a part of me and not just a possession I own.

~ Susan Keen Krontz

After the candle was lit and I placed my hands on the eyes and said the invocation, I felt energy in my crown; I also felt a lightness of heart. I felt very moved. I wanted to cry a bit. I still want to cry writing this. I think what I felt was the energy of the Gods. It was a beautiful, pure energy that seemed to filter through my heart. It was a really beautiful experience.

~ Salisha Noor-Birjou

There was an aura (light yellow to golden) around the candle and the flame for most of the time. I also heard noises to my left and there was absolutely no one there, not even my dogs. Once everything was finished, I picked up my cards and began shuffling them. They felt so light in my hands. Overall, I had a good feeling about it and can't wait to use it for healing and magic!

~ Aristea Athanasiou

Activation of the Deck for Healing and Magic

I noticed that when I cleaned everything up, that as I picked up the deck, it felt very heavy. Like it carried a lot of substance. I am sure you understand what I mean when I say that the deck didn't feel negative heavy but felt...heavy.

~ Evie Nance

The candle became lighter when the cleansing process was complete and again heavier when charged. Now my cards are wonderful; I am not sure whether they feel heavier...maybe just a tad and I really have not used them since. I am looking forward to using them in healing others, which I feel is my path and mission in life. I have felt a connection with my cards since receiving them and it is stronger now. So starts my new adventure with my cards. I am very excited to see where they lead me!"

~Jessica Olson

I found this to be a very simple but very powerful ritual. The power of the ritual was evident upon the first invocation. It manifested as a warm rush though my body and a feeling of well-being.

~ Keith Amarak

As I was reciting the prayer, I felt a peace come over my body, like a huge mountain lifting, I felt really good. The deck feels lighter to me now and I am much more aware of when to stop shuffling, whereas before, I wasn't confident when I stopped. I kept on thinking maybe I should have shuffled more. That's not the case now."

~ Marijana Georgiou

Towards the end of the second repetition, I noticed myself reciting from memory and closing my eyes at times. By the end of the third repetition, I became very aware of an energy on my left side. It was like standing next to a full-length mirror reflecting the candle light and my profile. There was intense energy running through the ground and my foot to my left hand, or vice versa, it was hard to tell. When I finished the fourth repetition, I was buzzing all over. I then reassembled the deck in numerical order. I began to shuffle the deck and I dropped it! I very much felt a presence and could see a woman smiling in my mind's eye, like having a little chuckle at me. Pretty sure it was Isis. So, I then started to shuffle the deck seven times again, this time a lot slower. My eyelids kept feeling heavy and my body was gently swaying, as I slowly shuffled. I think I may have even been humming a tune. On the fifth shuffle, a card jumped and I didn't freak this time and just picked it up and placed it in and continued shuffling, I did note that it was the God card that had jumped. Then on the next shuffle, another card jumped! I picked it up and placed it back in the deck and saw it was the Goddess card! I gave the deck one more shuffle and then placed it in front of the purple candle while it continued to burn."

~ Sama Rose

It is my hope that when you undertake the Activation Ceremony for your own deck that you will not only enjoy the process, but also perhaps experience something profound.

HEALTH AND HEALING

Many readers do not consider it wise to read about health-related issues due to the fact that many people would prefer to consult a card reader about their health rather than to visit a doctor who is a qualified professional when it comes to health matters. The Lenormand cards, however, have a long-standing association with health. The Tree card, for instance, can represent a person's health when it appears in a reading, with surrounding cards providing additional details. Whether you decide to read on your own or someone else's health, keep this in mind: If you do the large spread, known as the Grand Tableau, for which all 36 cards of a traditional Lenormand deck are used, you are going to be seeing The Tree card, so naturally information about health will appear somewhere in the reading.

Personally, I do not accept health-related questions from clients, especially if I already know they have yet to consult a doctor. Should someone have a very serious illness for which they have been receiving treatment, or a chronic condition for which they have repeatedly consulted doctors, then I will read for them because, in those cases, I know this person is already under medical care. Otherwise, I recommend they consult a doctor first, then get a card reading once they have been properly diagnosed. I do not recommend ever using the Lenormand or any other system of divination to arrive at a possible diagnosis.

Traditionally, each Lenormand card has been associated with a particular body part or ailment by European Lenormand readers for many years (Treppner, 2013). After extensively using the Lenormand when reading for members of the health profession for a number of years, Andy Boroveshengra (2014) arrived at a number of health-related meanings and interpretations. Another source I am including is the work of Sylvie Steinbach (2007), who also associates each card with certain health issues and body parts.

I strongly urge you to choose one of these sources and adhere to that particular source for use of their health-related card meanings because they do vary on a number of the cards. Do not pick and choose and combine the meanings of more than one scholar when you are interpreting a reading. Read through this portion of the chapter and decide which meanings seem to resonate with you the best, then always stick to those meanings.

Personally, I resonate best with the health meanings provided by Andy Boroveshengra (2014) simply because his blog was a primary source of mine as I was learning how to read Lenormand cards. However, you may resonate better with Treppner (2013) or Steinbach's (2007) health meanings.

As you will quickly discover through the use of this deck, *The Egyptian Lenormand* is not a typical Lenormand deck of divination. Considering that I channeled all of the card images from divine beings, those energies we know today as the gods of ancient Egypt, there is more to each image than just its traditional divinatory meaning that derives from the Lenormand system of divination. These images, when you undertake the Activation Ceremony, become conduits of energy from the gods that can then be accessed and used in order to channel healing energy as well as the energy of manifestation. This chapter concludes with my method as to how *The Egyptian Lenormand* can be used in order to channel healing energy for yourself and others.

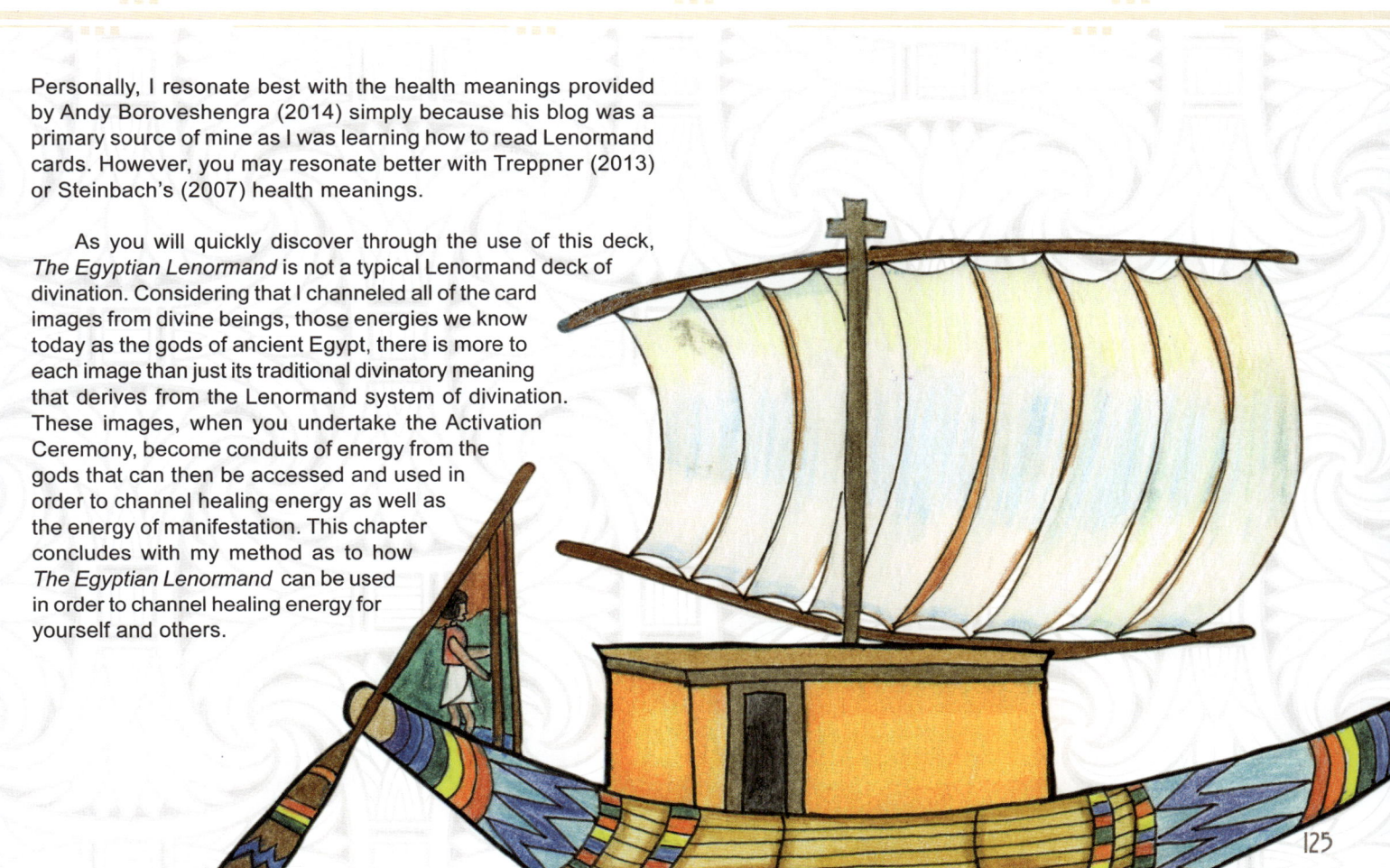

HEALTH AND HEALING

HEALTH ASSOCIATIONS

1. RIDER

The Rider is a depiction of a Bedouin man on a camel on the Giza Plateau. Camels were a very important mode of transportation in ancient Egypt. The Rider card represents a messenger, or news coming to you. A young man on a horse is what is depicted on traditional Lenormand Rider cards. Due to the associations with travel and movement, The Rider card has traditionally become associated with the lower extremities: legs, knees, and feet (Boroveshengra, 2014: 5; Steinbach 2007:8) and also with the ligaments (Boroveshengra, 2014:15; Treppner 2013: Loc. 140). When asking questions related to health, should Rider appear, this card may indicate an issue with a person's legs or issues with ligaments somewhere in the body. Physical mobility may be problematic.

2. CLOVER

I chose to depict Egyptian Clover as the Clover card for my deck, along with the River Nile and a pyramid in the background. Traditional Lenormand decks have a depiction of a clover plant as well, usually with just some very basic bucolic background images, while the clover plant itself is up front and center, being the main symbol on the card. The Clover indicates a short period of good luck, a happy opportunity, albeit short-lived. Regarding health issues, The Clover can indicate dietary concerns ranging from a need for additional iron (Treppner 2013: Loc. 148) to foods a person needs to add to their diet in order to increase their intake of minerals (Boroveshengra, 2014:16), but mainly, The Clover is seen as a card indicating healing (Boroveshengra, 2014:16; Treppner, 2013). According to Steinbach (2007:11), the Clover card can signify the aura.

3. SHIP

According to Boroveshengra (2014:18), the Ship is a card of movement and is associated with such illnesses. Depicting travel across water, it is only logical that The Ship can indicate sea-sickness and motion sickness; therefore, nausea is indicated. Areas of the body governed by The Ship are the pancreas, liver, gallbladder, and spleen (Boroveshengra 2014:18; Steinbach 2007:15).

4. HOUSE

When one dreams of a house, as a dream symbol it is interpreted as representing the human body. The house is a physical structure, just as the human body is also a physical structure created to house the soul. Consequently, the House card has come to be associated with the skeletal structure of the human body (Boroveshengra 2014:21; Steinbach 2007:20).

5. TREE

The card of health itself, The Tree also represents the family and one's ancestral lineage; therefore, The Tree can also be indicative of particular health issues that are of a chronic or hereditary nature (Boroveshengra, 2014). Steinbach (2007:23) relates The Tree to mental health and the brain while Treppner (2013: Loc. 175) suggests a person needs to spend more time out in nature. The Tree card is an excellent example of how all three Lenormand scholars can differ on the health associations of a single card.

HEALTH AND HEALING

6. CLOUDS

The Clouds card represents the lungs and respiratory health in general (Boroveshengra 2014:22; Steinbach 2007:28; Treppner 2013: Loc. 186).

7. SNAKE

Due to the twisting and winding nature of the snake's body, this card has long been associated with digestive health; and in particular, the large and small intestines (Boroveshengra 2014:23; Steinbach 2007:34).

8. SARCOPHAGUS

Traditionally known as The Coffin card, the Sarcophagus signifies an illness that is particularly severe and causes you to take to your bed as you are unable to participate in your usual daily activities (Boroveshengra 2014:24). Steinbach (2007:38), on the other hand, associates this card with the end of the intestines and the colon. Treppner (2013: Loc. 203) states this card may indicate headaches or low energy levels.

Author Note: In my own readings, I have seen the Sarcophagus appear when someone has had to remain in bed due to being very ill. It can also refer to hospitalization; therefore, I follow Boroveshengra's (2014:24) interpretation, as I have seen that play out time and time again in card readings.

9. FLOWERS

Also known as Bouquet in other Lenormand decks, the Flowers card in a reading related to health issues is a card of healing and recovery (Boroveshengra 2014:25). This makes logical sense because Flowers is interpreted as meaning a gift and happiness. What greater gift than to be healed from an ailment? Also, when friends and loved ones are ill, it is customary to give them a bouquet of flowers in order to help lift their spirits. Steinbach (2007:41) relates the card to the hair and face while Treppner (2013: Loc. 214) suggests that natural remedies are called for as a method of treatment.

10. SICKLE

Also known as Scythe in other Lenormand decks, the Sickle is a card of cutting and separation. Therefore, it is associated with cuts, abrasions, and wounds that break the skin. Both Boroveshengra (2014:26) and Treppner (2013: Loc. 221) link this card to a cut, the need to consult a dentist, or surgery. Steinbach (2007:49) relates this card to the mouth and teeth.

11. CROOK & FLAIL

Known in other Lenormand decks as Whips, Rod, or Broom, The Crook & Flail card is associated with arguments and harsh words. Regarding health issues, Crook & Flail has come to be associated with ailments pertaining to the throat or the ability to speak (Boroveshengra 2014:28). Treppner (2013: Loc.

HEALTH AND HEALING

232) also associates this card with the throat, while Steinbach (2007:50) differs greatly by associating the card with the tendons, muscles, and the penis.

12. BIRDS

Known as a card signifying gossip, both Boroveshengra (2014:29) and Treppner (2013: Loc. 239) associate the Birds card with stress; whereas, Steinbach (2007:54) associates this card with the throat and speech due to its strong association with communication. Boroveshengra (2014:29) also associates the Birds with the eyes, an association that has played out in my own personal readings.

Author Note: For a few months I repeatedly received the card combination of Tree + Birds when reading for myself. At first, I took this to indicate communication with family members. Well, that is a fairly common occurrence, so I could not figure out why the Lenormand cards would keep bringing this to my attention. I then began to view the Tree in terms of health, so something about my health and the Birds card connection to my health was being indicated. When I first realized the connection, I was just developing a sinus infection that began as a sore throat, so I thought, aha! The Birds is connected to the throat; therefore, my readings have been telling me to be careful of my health with regards to my throat.

As time went on and I healed from that sinus infection, the card combination of Tree + Birds kept appearing in my readings. Upon further research, I discovered that Boroveshengra (2014:29) states that The Birds card relates to the eyes. I have a long history of ocular hypertension, which can be a precursor to glaucoma. My mother had a serious case of glaucoma and eventually lost the sight in her right eye. I grew increasingly worried as this card combination kept appearing, so I scheduled an appointment with a specialist after not seeing an eye doctor in three years. After a rigorous examination, the doctor saw evidence of optic nerve damage, so now I am receiving proper treatment. Had I not taken note of the card combination of

Tree + Birds repeatedly appearing in my readings, and had I not made the effort to further research the health meaning of the Birds card, I may never have gone to see an eye specialist until it was too late and the disease too far advanced for the simpler treatments to be effective. Once I saw the eye specialist, the card combination of Tree + Birds vanished from my readings.

My experience is a wonderful example not only of the accuracy of the Lenormand system of divination, but also of the importance of noting repeating card combinations in readings as possessing added significance.

13. CHILD

Simply put, since the Child is a young person, this card represents any type of childhood illness like measles, mumps, and chicken pox (Boroveshengra 2014:30; Treppner 2013:Loc. 250). Steinbach associates the Child card with the breasts and chest (2007:59).

14. DESERT FOX

Known simply as the Fox in other Lenormand decks, the Desert Fox is known for its acute sense of smell; therefore, the Desert Fox card is associated with the nose, things that smell wrong (for example, infection or rotten food), and with the Tree can even indicate the possibility of an incorrect diagnosis (Boroveshengra 2014:31) and the need for a second opinion. Steinbach (2007:63) also associates this card with the nose and sense of smell, while Treppner (2013: Loc. 246) suggests that this card be viewed as a warning and may indicate an incorrect diagnosis.

HEALTH AND HEALING

15. SACRED COW

The cow has four compartments within its stomach, and Sacred Cow (known as Bear in other Lenormand decks) is associated with the stomach and stomach issues (Steinbach 2007:68). Boroveshengra (2014:32) relates this card to physical strength and endurance. Treppner (2013: Loc. 263) associates this card with stress and the need to slow down.

16. STARS

The ancient Egyptians saw the stars as the glorified ancestors who ascended into the heavens in order to join the gods. Here, on my version of the Stars card, they cover the body of the sky goddess, Nut, who is also associated with the nighttime sky. The Stars card is seen as associated with the night and with sleep. Boroveshengra (2014:33) associates the Stars card with sleep disorders and also to the cells within the human body. Steinbach (2007:71) links the Stars card to the skin.

17. IBIS

Known as the Stork or Storks in other Lenormand decks, it's obvious that both the stork and ibis have very long legs. Consequently, this card has come to be associated with the legs (Boroveshengra 2014:34; Steinbach 2007:75).

18. DOG

The card of faithfulness and friendship, here Anubis is depicted. Anubis is a psychopomp, a deity who helps guide the dead through the perils of the Duat, the Egyptian underworld. Regarding health issues, the Dog card is associated with the sense of taste and the tongue (Steinbach 2007:79) and Boroveshengra (2014:35) adds that the Dog may also represent a health care professional.

19. OBELISK

Known as the Tower in other Lenormand decks, the Obelisk is a tall, imposing, and straight edifice created for the sole purpose of glorifying the achievements of the pharaohs. This card has come to be associated with the back and the spine (Steinbach 2007:86 and Treppner 2013:Loc. 300), while Boroveshengra (2014:36) also associates this card with longevity.

20. GARDEN

Socializing and meeting in public places are two interpretations of the Garden card. When it comes to health-related issues, the Garden can therefore represent a location where you go in order to be healed or to recuperate from an illness, such as a rehabilitation facility or hospital (Boroveshengra 2014:40; Treppner 2013:Loc. 307). Since the Garden often can indicate meeting others in a social setting, I have seen it appear in readings to represent contagious diseases, such as the flu and viruses, especially when paired with Clouds, which can indicate a communicable respiratory illness like the flu or viral bronchitis (see also Boroveshengra 2014:22).

HEALTH AND HEALING

21. MOUNTAIN

Representing a major obstacle, lengthy delay, or perhaps a powerful enemy, when it comes to health issues the Mountain can indicate a lengthy illness (Treppner 2013:Loc. 318). Steinbach (2007:94) associates the mountain with the head; whereas, Boroveshengra (2014:38) is even more specific and links the Mountain with blockages, stenosis, and calcification affecting the head.

22. CROSSROADS

Also known as Roads and Paths in other Lenormand decks, the Crossroads are the roads and highways upon which we travel. Within the human body, this imagery is interpreted as the system of veins and arteries along which our blood flows (Boroveshengra 2014:39; Steinbach 2007:98, Treppner 2013: Loc. 325).

23. MICE

Mice can indicate anxiety and worry that eat away at us; therefore, this card is connected to the human nervous system (Steinbach 2007:101), as well as parasites and other types of illnesses that can consume us from the inside out, such as ulcers and tumors (Boroveshengra 2014:40).

24. HEART

The Heart card obviously represents the actual physical heart and cardiovascular health in general. Boroveshengra (2014:41) also points out that when paired with Birds, this card combination can indicate high blood pressure or some type of heart arrhythmia.

25. RING

The Ring is in the shape of a circle. The circle represents eternity because it has no beginning and no end. Regarding health issues, it can represent the simultaneous existence of two illnesses (Boroveshengra 2014:42), chronic conditions (Treppner 2013: Loc. 349), and the lymphatic system (Steinbach 2007:112).

26. SCROLL

The Scroll is known as The Book in other Lenormand decks. Based upon its strong connection to education and learning, the Scroll represents the brain in a reading (Boroveshengra 2014:43; Steinbach 2007:116) and psychological illnesses (Treppner 2013:Loc. 360).

HEALTH AND HEALING

27. LETTER

The Letter in a reading represents a written document; therefore, in matters of health, it often signifies a prescription or some other diagnostic write up, perhaps the results of a test (Treppner 2013: Loc. 367; Boroveshengra 2014:44) and can be connected with the health of the hands (Boroveshengra 2014:44; Steinbach 2007:119), since in the old days letters were always written by hand.

28./29. GOD AND GODDESS/PHARAOH AND PRIESTESS

These cards signify the person receiving the reading, whether yourself, a friend, or client. Boroveshengra (2014) and Steinbach (2007) do not associate either card with any health or body issues. Treppner (2013:Loc. 374) links the Man card (the God and Pharaoh cards in *The Egyptian Lenormand*) with "small wounds." Treppner (2013:Loc. 381) further associates the Woman card (Goddess and Priestess) with the hormones.

30. WATER LILY

Known as Lily or Lilies in other Lenormand decks, the Water Lily represents peace, harmony, wisdom, and maturity. Due to this flower's pronounced stamens, it is viewed by readers as having a phallic nature. Based upon that, Treppner (2013:Loc. 388) and Boroveshengra (2014:47) connect this card to all illnesses with a sexual component, including sexually transmitted diseases and sexual dysfunction. Steinbach (2007:132) connects this card to the eyes and ears, also the senses of sight and hearing.

Author Note: Boroveshengra (2014:47) goes on to say that when this card appears in a reading, it can sometimes represent people who care for the elderly. I began reading Lenormand when my mother became very ill in her old age and she was under the care of doctors and nurses for the final 13 months of her life. This card would often appear in readings about her as representing the healthcare staff. I have also seen this card represent hospice care in a reading when my father was dying. Although Boroveshengra (2014) states that this particular association is very rare, please be aware that if you know of someone receiving hospital, rehab, or nursing home care, chances are good that this card pertains to the care they are receiving or to the facility itself in which they are housed.

31. SUN

All three sources connect the Sun card to physical energy of an individual (Boroveshengra 2014:48; Steinbach 2007:137; Treppner 2013:Loc. 399). It's important when the Sun appears in a reading about health to also examine nearby cards because those will help determine if something is bringing down a person's energy levels or if something the surrounding cards represent can be used to help increase stamina. Treppner (2013:Loc. 399) goes on to say that intense self-care and pampering may also be required in order for the person to return to their former sense of stamina. Steinbach (2007:137) further connects this card with the solar plexus chakra, which is located at the base of the breast bone and governs a person's sense of willpower and determination, so again, there is a connection to one's physical stamina.

32. MOON

The Moon is seen by pagan religions as being feminine and representative of the Goddess; therefore, the Moon in a reading about health will be referencing female reproductive issues, hormones, the breasts, and the necessity of attempting to keep such factors in balance (Boroveshengra 2014:49: Steinbach 2007:142). The Moon card can also indicate the personal rhythms of the person being read (Treppner 2013: Loc. 406).

33. KEY

The Key represents success; however, all three sources differ on how it is seen for readings pertaining to health. Boroveshengra (2014:50) views the Key as indicative of tests and diagnoses. Treppner (2013:Loc. 416), on the other hand, views the Key as representing a successful outcome to any illness or medical procedure. Steinbach (2007:146) has a much more esoteric view of the Key and connects it with the third-eye chakra and also the soul.

34. FISH

Due to the fact that fish live underwater, all three sources connect the Fish card to the kidneys, bladder, and urinary system (Boroveshengra 2014:51; Steinbach 2007:149; Treppner 2013: Loc. 423). Treppner also associates The Fish with the blood and the necessity of keeping the blood free of contaminates (2013: Loc. 423–Loc. 427), and mentions alcohol, while Boroveshengra (2014) states that the Fish card can represent alcoholism and also sperm.

35. ANCHOR

The Anchor represents stability in a reading; therefore, both Boroveshengra (2014:52) and Steinbach (2007:153) associate the Anchor with the pelvis and hips. Treppner (2013: Loc. 433) associates this card with over-indulgence and the need to limit sweets.

36. DJED PILLAR

Known as The Cross in other Lenormand decks, in Egyptian mythology the djed pillar represents the lower spine of the god, Osiris. All three sources associate this card with the lower back, or lumbar region when it appears in a health reading (Boroveshengra 2014:53; Steinbach 2007:157; Treppner 2013: Loc. 445).

37. CAT

The Cat is a non-traditional card that many modern Lenormand deck creators are adding to their decks. The Cat represents agility and alertness. When the Cat appears in a reading about health, it represents problems with mobility, stiff joints, decreased comprehension, and due to so many people being allergic to cats, the Cat card can also represent asthmatic and bronchial issues (Den Elder, personal communication, 2013).

HEALTH AND HEALING

CHANNELING HEALING ENERGY

Every image of *The Egyptian Lenormand* was channeled directly from the Egyptian deities with whom I work—most notably: Isis, Khepera, Bastet, Thoth, and Anubis. I was told in the very beginning that the cards would go beyond divination. The images would be conduits for healing and magical energies. A deck of cards is just that: a deck of cards. They are images printed on cardstock that do not contain any inherent energy or magic at all. *The Egyptian Lenormand* differs only due to the Activation Ceremony. Once you perform the Activation Ceremony with your deck, the cards come alive with the energies that were placed into each image by the gods as I rendered those images on paper. If you wish to use the cards for healing and magic you must carry out the Activation Ceremony, then your deck is ready for further specialized uses unique to *The Egyptian Lenormand*.

Please note that when using these cards for healing, or combined with any other healing modalities, such as Reiki, for example, it is strongly advised that you do not do this in isolation. Be sure to consult with a medical professional and obtain an accurate diagnosis. Never use the Lenormand or any other system of divination in order to diagnose yourself or another person. Be responsible and consult with a healthcare professional first. Once you have a diagnosis then you can begin to use your cards to facilitate your own healing process while you are under medical care.

The Egyptian Lenormand cards can be used to focus healing energy for yourself, a loved one, friends, and even pets and the environment. The person can be present or not, it makes no difference. Energy knows no geographic distances or boundaries, so the energies can be used to conduct healing energy long distance. You do not have to be a practitioner of any other type of healing modality in order to use *The Egyptian Lenormand* to channel healing energies yourself. The healing energies are all self-contained within the symbols that appear within the images of the cards and become activated as conduits as a result of the Activation Ceremony and when used with the proper focus and intent.

There are two methods for using the cards to channel healing energies. The first is for in-person sessions during which you are working on yourself or another person and you are both together in the same room. The second method varies from the first and is intended to help you to focus and channel healing energies long distance. When using these cards in this manner, refer to the earlier portion of this chapter for the body and illness associations of the cards. Also remember to choose one scholar's approach and follow their approach for each card. Do not combine approaches. The cards will work better for you if you decide to use either Boroveshengra (2014), Steinbach (2007), or Treppner's (2013) health associations for the cards.

METHOD FOR IN-PERSON SESSIONS

You will need the full deck of cards, both Eye of Horus Activation cards, and if you wish to use incense or a candle for additional atmosphere, you may feel free to do so. When using incense, please keep in mind that the scent of frankincense and myrrh is sacred to the deities of ancient Egypt. I highly recommend that be the scent you use; however, other scents that also work well are sandalwood and rose.

When you embark upon a healing session, make sure you will remain uninterrupted. Turn your phone off and be sure if you have children or pets that they do not interrupt the process.

The recipient of the energy should be dressed in comfortable and loose clothing. You may wish to have a light blanket on hand in case the recipient becomes chilly during the session. Ideally, you should not consume any red meat, alcohol, or caffeine the twenty-four hours prior to the session because, when taken into the body, the energy level, or vibration of a person, is lowered as a result of ingesting them.

Prepare your space by making sure the recipient has a comfortable chair to sit in or couch or bed to lie on. For the actual session, position the recipient so that you will be able to stand to their left in order to channel healing energy into their energy field during the session. The human body takes in energy from the left and sends it outward from the right. This is the reason behind the practitioner standing to the left of the recipient.

Upon discussing with the recipient their maladies, you can then search the deck for the cards that represent those illnesses or the affected body parts. If there is a card for the affected body part and another card that represents the illness you may use both cards, if you so desire.

Remove the card(s) signifying the illness from the deck and place them side by side, face up. Place the first Eye of Horus Activation card to the left and the other to the right of the cards. You should now have anywhere from three to five cards all lined up from left to right. As with the Activation Ceremony, there is brief prayer you should say before conducting the session. You can say the prayer either aloud or to yourself, it doesn't matter. You begin by placing your hands, palms downward, over the cards. You can rest your hands directly on the cards or hold your hands just above the cards—it doesn't matter. Do whichever makes you feel the most comfortable. The prayer is as follows:

Isis, Great Physician and Mistress of Healing,

I call upon You on behalf of [state "myself" if for you, name of recipient if for someone else]

I ask that You channel Your healing energy

Through these cards and into the physical body,

Through these cards and into the emotional body,

Through these cards and into the mental body,

HEALTH AND HEALING

Through these cards and into the spiritual body.

I ask that You grant necessary healing on all levels

So that wholeness and health may be restored.

I ask this of You, Mighty Isis, in Your holy name,

AMEN.

RECLINING SESSION

If the person receiving the energy is lying down, carefully place all the cards on their body. Begin with the first Eye of Horus card and place it on the person's heart chakra in the center of their chest, so that the card is oriented vertically on the person's body. Next, place the card(s) that represent(s) the malady directly beneath the Eye of Horus card so you create a line of cards moving down from the person's heart chakra toward their navel. When done, place the final Eye of Horus card beneath the last card signifying the illness.

Place your right hand on the left shoulder of the recipient in preparation for channeling the healing energy into their aura. At this point repeat the prayer to Isis a second time.

Next, pick up the cards in the same order in which you placed them on the recipient. Pass them to the left hand of the recipient and have them hold the cards against their heart chakra. Both Eye of Horus cards should be sandwiching the cards representing the illness between them. Place your right hand again on their left shoulder and repeat the prayer to Isis a third time.

As you repeat the prayer a third time, visualize iridescent green light coming down from the heavens and entering the top of your own head. Feel the energy pulsate and flow through your body and out through your right hand. Visualize the healing energy enter the recipients left shoulder and imagine it slowly spreading through the person's entire body from head to toe. Remember to keep your right hand on the recipient's left shoulder during the entire process.

Once you have visualized the healing energy filling their entire body, repeat the prayer to Isis a fourth and final time. The energy may still be flowing, so stand with your right hand on their left shoulder and continue the visualization. See the energy with your mind's eye flowing down from the universe into the top of your head, out through your right hand, and into the recipient's left shoulder and through their body down to their toes.

When you feel ready, you may conclude the session. At this point, you should give thanks in your own words to Isis and any other beings of light who may have helped in the process.

As you conclude, make slow sweeping gestures from head to toe along the person's body. This is a practice from Reiki and is called "brushing the aura." It helps to settle the newly introduced healing energies into the chakras and aura of the recipient.

Use your own intuition to judge when the brushing process is complete. It's usually very quick and typically takes five to ten seconds. The session is now complete.

Have the recipient drink a full glass of water to help in the release of toxins from the physical and etheric bodies. As the channel of the healing energy, you have also received a healing session, so it is advised that you also drink a full glass of water to facilitate in your own healing process.

CHAIR SESSION

If the person is seated in a chair, after arranging the cards on your altar or table top and saying the opening prayer, merely hand them each card being sure they remain in the same order. They are to carefully hold the cards in their hands so that the two Eye of Horus Activation cards sandwich between them the card(s) that represent their illness as they bow their head. At this point, place your right hand on their left shoulder and repeat the prayer a second time.

The recipient is then to bring the cards up to their heart chakra, located at the center of the chest, and hold the cards gently against their heart chakra and close their eyes. They are to continue holding the cards in that position against the heart chakra until the session is complete.

At this point, while keeping your right hand on the recipient's left shoulder, repeat the prayer to Isis a third time. Imagine iridescent, green healing light flowing down from the heavens and into the top of your own head. Feel the energy slowly course through your entire body from head to toe, and then out of your right hand. Envision the healing energy entering the left shoulder of the recipient and visualize it slowly entering their body flowing up to the head, then down through the rest of the body to the toes.

Once you have visualized the healing energy flowing through the entire body of the recipient, repeat the prayer to Isis for the fourth and final time. Feel the energy flowing from the universe through your body, out through your right hand and into the recipient's left shoulder and through their entire body. At this point you are ready to conclude the session. Use your best judgment or intuition as to when you feel the energy flow begins to slow or dissipate. As it does, give thanks in your own words and make slow sweeping gestures along the recipient's body to slowly brush the aura from head to toe along the front and back of the body. This helps to settle the energy into the chakras and aura.

The session is now complete. Once again, have the recipient drink a full glass of water, as well as yourself.

A SELF-HEALING SESSION FOR YOURSELF

The methodology is the same, except that you do not place your right hand on your own left shoulder. When you cross arms over your body from one side to the other, that breaks the flow of energy. Instead of doing that, simply imagine Isis standing to your left with her right hand on your left shoulder.

HEALTH AND HEALING

Sandwich the cards together with the first Eye of Horus Activation card as the top of the sandwich and the second Eye of Horus Activation card as the bottom of the sandwich. In between will be the cards that represent the malady and/or related body parts. Hold the cards up against your heart chakra at the center of your chest. Go through the visualization as detailed above and repeat the prayer to Isis at the appropriate times. When you are done, you may brush your own aura from the top of your head downward to your feet. Remember to drink a full glass of water immediately afterwards.

LONG DISTANCE SESSIONS

Energy knows no geographic boundaries, and it can also move through Time as well, hence this is why healing sessions can also work on the spiritual or karmic level. Therefore, it is only a matter of changing the intention behind your healing session that will allow you to also send the energy over vast geographic distances to recipients anywhere in the world.

The methodology varies only slightly.

Begin by first agreeing with the recipient upon a particular date and time for their session. Do make note of any differences in the time zones and coordinate your session accordingly. Instruct the recipient via email or phone the same way as you would a person who comes to you for an in-person session. Make note of their particular health concerns so you can use this knowledge when you pull cards for their session. Be sure to advise them to drink a full glass of water after their session is complete and the importance of taking steps to be sure they are not interrupted during their session.

In order to channel energy for someone who is not physically present, there are two main methods. For the first method, you simply use your own body as the substitute, but you are channeling the energy with the intention in your mind of sending it to the intended recipient. As the channel, you will always receive healing as well, since the energy needs to pass through your entire body before it can enter the body of the recipient. Follow the instructions for the Self-Healing Session for Yourself.

A second method of sending long distance energy consists of using a surrogate to represent the recipient. Feel free to use a stuffed animal or a doll, but if it is a stuffed animal, a teddy bear is ideal because it had a head, shoulders, arms, legs, and torso like a human's. You would then focus on the doll or stuffed animal as if it were the recipient there in person with you with the exception of what you do with the cards after you have laid them out for the session.

Decide ahead of time if you will be using your own body or a surrogate to represent the recipient. A few minutes prior to the agreed-upon time of the session write the person's full name, date of birth, and location on a slip of paper. Have an area set up in advance where you will lay out the cards you will use. Prior to their session, go over their list of maladies and choose the cards that signify those maladies or body parts. Also set aside both Eye of Horus Activation cards.

Begin the session as you would an in-person session. Lay the cards out from left to right with the first Eye of Horus Activation card on the left, the card(s) signifying the maladies next, and conclude with the second Eye of Horus Activation card on the right.

Take the slip of paper with the recipient's information written upon it and place it on the first Eye of Horus Activation card. The first Eye of Horus Activation card opens the stream of energy.

Read their full information aloud seven times. This creates an energetic link between you and the recipient that begins the session.

Say the prayer to Isis.

If you are using a doll or stuffed animal to substitute for the absent recipient, after placing their information on the first Eye of Horus Activation card and reading their name seven times, place the slip of paper on the toy and again; repeat the recipient's information seven times in order to create an energetic link between the recipient and the toy you are using to represent them. Repeat the prayer at this point.

If you are acting as the surrogate for the recipient carry out the remainder of the session as you would for a self-healing, but be sure when you gather up and sandwich the cards together that you also include the slip of paper with the recipient's information written upon it. Hold the cards against your heart chakra for the duration of the session and remember to brush your own aura afterwards and also drink a full glass of water because you would have also received energy.

If you are using a toy as a surrogate, follow the instructions for a Reclining Session. Due to the small size of the doll or stuffed toy you may sandwich the cards together and lay them, along with the recipient's information, on the middle of the doll or toy's torso instead of laying them all out along the torso. Continue the session as described previously.

POSSIBLE EXPERIENCES DURING AND AFTER A SESSION

Any type of healing session can dredge up things for which the recipient may be unprepared. It is always best that you discuss this with the intended recipient prior to the session. Some actually do change their minds once they have this information, but in my practice this has only occurred twice.

The healing energy channeled to you via the symbols contained within the images of *The Egyptian Lenormand* heals on all levels: physical, emotional, mental, and spiritual. When I use the term "spiritual," I am referring to those ailments that affect a person on the soul level, such as unresolved past-life issues, physical traumas that occurred in past lives that a person has brought forward with them into their current physical incarnation, and cases of what is termed "soul loss," which is the situation in which someone has been so severely traumatized in the past that they left a piece of their soul in that location.

HEALTH AND HEALING

The healing energy channeled by you via the symbols on these cards can help to bring some relief regarding many issues, but again, never use *The Egyptian Lenormand* or any type of divination or alternative healing as a substitute for professional medical help from healthcare professionals.

The healing energy works on the etheric, or energy, body. The energy is carried along the seven main chakras and flows through the meridians to all points of the physical body, and then flows around the physical body to also infuse the aura with healing energy.

When receiving a healing session, the recipient (this includes yourself, as well) may feel one or more of the following sensations:

- **Heat or just a sense of increased warmth**
- **A tingling or prickly sensation, particularly in a body part that has sustained an injury at some point in time**
- **Chills (hence the importance of keeping a light blanket on hand)**
- **A sense of peace**
- **Lightheadedness**
- **Extreme sleepiness (many do fall asleep during a session)**
- **A strong urge to urinate (so the session may have to be interrupted)**
- **Additional hands on your body that are not physically present**

While receiving a healing session, I have felt each of these sensations at one time or another. Most commonly, I feel heat, but again this will vary from individual to individual, plus it also varies based upon how the energy is working for you. Be prepared to feel something, yet in some cases individuals feel nothing at all.

Once the healing session is complete it can take several days for the energy to settle into your own energy field, so the healing work is ongoing. Through my own practice and asking my clients later how they have felt, the average consensus is that after-effects can be felt off and on for as long as a week.

What I tell my clients is that a healing session works to cleanse your body, chakras, and auras of physical, emotional, mental, and spiritual toxins. It's the same principle when we take antibiotics for an infection. The medication fights the germs that are causing the infection, but the patient may feel stomach upset or some other types of digestive discomfort as a result. The same applies to a healing session.

Most people have reported that once they have gone home or a day or two has passed, they will experience an uncontrollable crying jag. It seems that nothing in particular sets them off. They just start crying and cannot seem to stop themselves as quickly as they would like. A crying jag is a result of receiving healing on the emotional level. Most of us have been hurt emotionally many times. We have failed relationships and some of us have been unfortunate enough to suffer abuse from another that results in carrying that emotional trauma forward through our life. A crying jag is the release of such traumas. If you find you are experiencing a crying jag, my best advice is to just allow it to flow. Should it occur and you are at work or in some public setting, I would recommend walking quickly to the nearest restroom and lock yourself in a stall; then let it out. It is quite unhealthy to hold it in and holding a crying jag in and preventing it from having its release can actually make you physically ill (usually with a sudden bad headache or severe stomach upset).

Sudden bursts of anger have also been experienced as an aftereffect of a healing session. The anger comes from receiving energy that works on the emotional level, but this can also sometimes be karmic as well, especially if you have been repeatedly victimized or persecuted in your past lives. Once again, as with the crying jag, just let it out. Scream into a pillow or beat it up. Do not allow the anger to remain within and fester. This would be very detrimental to your overall health and emotional outlook.

Other aftereffects you or the recipient may feel after a session include, but are not limited to:

- Dizziness or lightheadedness

- Temporary blurred vision

- Ongoing tingling or heat in a body part that has experienced physical trauma

- Extreme tiredness and the need to sleep

- Nausea (sometimes accompanied by actual vomiting, but this is very rare)

- Aches or ongoing heat in a particular chakra location

All of this is normal and is nothing to be alarmed about. All of these sensations are temporary and most will fade within an hour of the session; however, some can linger and be felt off and on for as long as a week, with the exceptions of the sleepiness and the nausea, which both fade well within an hour and do not appear to reoccur.

SUMMARY

In conclusion, *The Egyptian Lenormand* becomes a valuable channel of healing energy once the Activation Ceremony has been performed. After the Activation Ceremony you are able to use the cards in order to channel healing energies for yourself and others, even over vast geographic distances. The energy works on all levels: physical, emotional, mental, and spiritual. All that is required of the recipient is that they approach the session with an open mind and are willing to receive whatever type of healing energy comes through for them.

The Power of Magic for Manifestation

In addition to their uses for divination and healing, *The Egyptian Lenormand* cards can also be used in manifestation work or magic (to use a more well-known term).

"Magic" isn't card tricks or sawing a lady in half. Nor is it instantaneous with miraculous results from twitching one's nose or lighting a few candles. As a magical practitioner with over thirty years of experience, I define magic as:

Directed focus, intention, and thought centering on a particular desired outcome.

Despite what you may read in books about magic, the only real "tools" that you need are:

- *A written and well-worded intention*
- *Your ability to focus*
- *The ability to maintain a single, sustained thought for a minute or two*

That is all.

You don't need candles, herbs, oils, poppets, or anything else. The best tool at your disposal is your mind. Additional tools—such as those noted above—help a person to focus or hold a sustained thought, like when you stare into a candle flame, but they are not intrinsically magical. The most magical of all tools is the human brain; therefore, *you* are the best tool that you possess and the real magic is within you.

Once you have performed the Activation Ceremony, the cards became not just mere pieces of cardstock with pretty pictures on them, but conduits of energy. In the previous chapter, I showed you how to use that energy in order to direct it for the intention to heal; in this chapter, I will focus on how you can use the cards to direct energy for manifestation, or "magic."

There are two things you must first know about magic/manifestation. To begin with, the intention behind the energy comes solely from the heart of the practitioner. Magic is the ability to focus your intention and thoughts toward a particular desired outcome; therefore, there is no "white" or "black." Intention is what classifies magic as for good or for ill, and intention resides within the heart. Magic is energy, just like electricity or the energy contained in a battery. It does its work without any conscious thoughts or feelings that it is doing good or harm.

Magic is therefore simply neutral. If one must assign magic a color, it would be gray as representative of its neutrality. Magic gains its positive or negative reputation based upon what is held in the heart of the practitioner (i.e., the type of intention) at the time the spell is performed. A person who always keeps in mind the highest good of all concerned when performing a spell, and never seeks to use the energy in order to attempt to manipulate or harm anyone, holds pure or high intentions; whereas, someone who directs energy and thought in order to control and manipulate others into doing things they would normally not do of their own free will, holds the intention to cause harm, and may deal with dark spiritual forces working with lower intentions. Intention is everything and it colors our thoughts, just as it also colors magical energy."

During my thirty years of being a magical practitioner, I have never seen a need to use magic in order to inflict harm or to manipulate a person's free will. What I tell my clients all the time is this: no matter the severity of the problem, there is always a way to deal with it that does not involve resorting to negative behavior. As long as your intentions are pure and are for the benefit of all involved, the ability to direct energy in order to manifest desired outcomes is a tremendous blessing for all concerned.

MAGICAL ETHICS

Whenever you perform magic, ethics need to be taken into account. As mentioned, magic is pure universal energy and, therefore, does not differentiate between white (good) and black (evil). Your intent and intentions color your magic, whether for good or bad. Your intent is the true you, the true feelings you have deep within your heart, your true motivation for performing a particular spell in the first place. There is no either/or in this situation. You are either coming from a good place when you perform magic, or you are not.

Magic with negative intentions usually comes in three main forms: purposefully using universal energy to cause harm to someone (and yes, this does include breaking up someone's existing relationship just because you want to be with them!), seeking revenge for either real or imagined wrongs against you or someone you love, and the purposeful inversion of any form of positive magic, including the Catholic Mass. By inversion, I mean the perversion of an existing ritual or religious practice by saying it backward and inverting sacred symbols upside-down, such as an inverted crucifix, which we've all seen in various horror movies, or saying "The Lord's Prayer" backwards.

When performing magic of any kind, always remember the Law of Three. Whatever you send out, will come back to you three times over. Basically, magic is energy; as such, once you let it loose, it will always come back to you, since you were the one to set it in motion. What goes around, comes around. So, if you request only good, then blessings will come back to you. However, if you perform magic with the intent to harm or manipulate others, then, in the end, you are only harming yourself.

When performing magic for yourself keep two questions in mind: do you truly feel what you desire to manifest is for your highest good; is it also for the highest good of all concerned (yourself, your family, children, and anyone else who may be involved in the situation)? If you can answer "yes" to both questions, then, by all means, proceed; however, keep in mind that God/dess, the Powers That Be, always know what is best for us, even when we are positive that the desired outcome would make our lives so much nicer, they may see something connected to it that would cause problems in the future. In order to protect you from those future problems, your spell may not work.

Yes, it's true. A magical practitioner does not always get what they ask for. If they did, well, I would have hit the lotto jackpot twenty years ago and I would be living in my dream house on the island of Maui in Hawaii. However, I am not. This is because candle work I have performed for myself in order to become wealthy has never worked. Despite that, I have all I need and all I desire, but in moderation in terms of the desired things. I am happy with that because I realize the gods know best. They will always have my (and your) best interests at heart. Never think just because a spell did not result in the desired outcome that the gods have ignored your request. No positive intention sent out into the universe goes to waste if you always include this caveat at the conclusion of every spell, which is:

"I ask for this, or something better."

That one simple statement then leaves it open for the gods to bring energies into motion that may not bring you exactly what you asked for, but will work to bring you something that will be along the same or similar lines—but even better for you in the long run.

As you begin to see results and become more proficient, of course you will wish to perform magic in order to help your family and friends. Just remember that energy is energy; and as such, once it is sent out it needs someone at the other end to be receptive to it, or the energy will simply dissipate into the universe. In other words, the person whom you are attempting to help needs to be aware of the energy you are going to be sending out on their behalf. Their conscious awareness of what you are doing for them is necessary in order for them to become open and receptive to receiving that energy into their life. If you go ahead and perform magic without the intended recipient being aware of what you are trying to do for them, you will not obtain the results you desire and the energy may not accomplish anything at all.

Conscious awareness behaves like a magnet. Once the intended person knows energy is being directed on their behalf for a particular wish or to help resolve a problem, they are then open to receiving the energy, so their own willingness to receive attracts the energy into their life so it can do the work you intended it to accomplish. When thinking of performing magic for others, please keep in mind not everyone is of like mind and some may be greatly offended or even horrified at the prospect. Therefore, use your own best judgment when offering to perform magic for others.

I would have to say that the most popular type of spell people have come to me for time and time again is for love. We all desire that one person who is meant for us and some people will go to great lengths to try to make that relationship a reality. Love magic has two intentions, and two intentions only: the intention to attract new love into your life, and the intention of strengthening an already-existing relationship, provided your partner is also willing to work things out.

You should never set your sights on a person and become convinced they are the one for you, and then attempt to use magic in order to manipulate that person into falling in love with you. A person must reciprocate your romantic interest in them. Otherwise, you have no business performing magic to attempt to force someone to fall in love with you, if that is not already within their free will to do so. This type of magic is manipulative because it undermines a person's free will, and if you had to assign a color to this type of magic, it would be black, very black. Besides, it's been my experience with clients who come to me after working with other magical practitioners that this type of manipulative and controlling love magic never works. The results, if any, wear off quickly and the person is left even more brokenhearted than they were in the beginning. I strongly caution you against using magical energy in order to force others to do your bidding. It may never work, or if it does work then it won't work for long, and you also establish some negative karma for yourself, so why bother with it?

Instead, it is fine to focus on attracting new love into your life, if that is what you desire. By so doing, you are focusing on having others see you in a more favorable light as more attractive, more charming, more interesting, and so on. In that way you are working on yourself first and not attempting to manipulate another person.

If you are interested in strengthening your already-existing relationship, that is perfectly permissible as well because your partner at one time or another made this commitment to you and to your relationship. However, I advise you to bear in mind should your partner no longer be willing to work on the relationship and is determined to leave, it may be best to allow them to leave with love instead of using magic in an attempt to manipulate them into staying with you. Again, such magic will not have lasting effects and you will end up feeling worse in the long run.

Magic is like medicine. Used according to the directions and with the best of intentions, it can bring about wonderful results. However, when used incorrectly for any reason, magic, like misused medication, can have very detrimental results. As long as you maintain high ethical standards, then your magic will always be guided by what you desire for your highest good and the highest good of all concerned. That is the ideal type of magic.

THE POWER OF MAGIC FOR MANIFESTATION

INTENTION, FOCUS, AND DIRECTED THOUGHT

The most important tools for any magical practitioner are intention, focus, and directed thought. You can have the freshest herbs, the highest grade of essential oils, and the nicest of candles, but if you are lacking with regards to your intentions, focus, or directed thought, then your spell will most likely not meet with much success.

Intention is basically what you are hoping to manifest into reality as a result of the performance of your spell. Intentions are written down. Ideally, you should write two copies in long-hand. Never type them. Writing them long-hand adds your own unique energy to the proceedings. Keep one copy for your journal (a magical journal is referred to in the literature as a "grimoire" or Book of Shadows) and the other you would place on your altar or in a prominent location in your personal sacred space.

When you word your intention, the manner in which you voice your desire is of the utmost importance. If you think about it, most of us were taught that when you desire to have something, you use the phrase: "I want." You may say, "I want some chocolate cake." However, if you look up the meaning for the word "want" in the dictionary, you will find that in its oldest verbal usage, the word "want" meant "to lack," as in to be missing or not possessing something you desire. When you use the phrase, "I want" when writing a magical intention, what you are saying to the universe is this: "I wish to lack …" whatever the object of your desire may be. For instance, if you'd like a new car you may incorrectly word your intention as: "I want a new car."

The universe would translate this simple phrase as: "I wish to lack a new car." This means that the new car may never enter your life.

Instead, strive to eliminate the word "want" from your vocabulary unless you are using it in its original form to mean "lack." Instead, substitute the words "wish" or "desire;" as in: "I desire a new car." Or, "I wish for a new car."

Intentions phrased using the words "wish" and "desire" are much more positive, plus in my three decades of experience as a magical practitioner, the words "wish" and "desire" garner much more positive results. Let's go over a few examples.

For instance, let's assume you have a problem with a co-worker who is constantly speaking badly of you to your supervisor and other co-workers and may also be attempting to take credit for your work. You wish to put a stop to this situation. In order to do that you may word your intention as:

I wish for Sarah to stop bad-mouthing me to others and cease from attempting to take credit for my work.

Another example: let's say you wish to strengthen an already-existing relationship. You could phrase your intention as:

> I wish for my relationship with Steven to become stronger, with us being more committed to one another.

A final example: let's say your child is being bullied at school and the school authorities fail to do anything about it, despite your numerous visits to the school to discuss the situation with the principal. You may phrase your magical intention as:

> I wish for Bobby to stop bullying Tom and for my son Tom to be surrounded by protective white light always.

The above example is a situation in which you can combine two different magical intentions. In this case, the intentions are to stop the bullying, while at the same time, generally protecting your child. Intentions can be combined only if they are related in some way to one another and are meant for the same person, as in the aforementioned example.

The next step is to write your intention down twice in long-hand. You can use any type of paper and ink that you please. There are no set rules, despite what you may read in books about Wicca and other types of magic. The most important thing to keep in mind is your intention must be hand-written.

Your intention is merely words on paper until you direct your focus and your own personal energy into it. If this is sounding complicated already, what follows at the end of this chapter is an example of a complete spell using *The Egyptian Lenormand* cards.

In order to place your own energy and focus into your intention, once it is written down you can hold the intention to your heart or your third eye (the third eye chakra is located at the center of the forehead just above the bridge of the nose and is the seat of intuition). Repeat the intention to yourself or out loud seven times. Seven is a number long held to be sacred and/or magical by a number of ancient cultures and civilizations, including the ancient Egyptians.

Once you have placed your energy into your intention and have focused upon it by repeating it seven times aloud or to yourself, you are ready for the next step, which consists of you directing your thought toward your desired outcome.

Let's return to an earlier example of hoping to get a new car. Your intention may read as:

> I wish to obtain a new car within the next 2 months that is easily affordable and is a dependable and enjoyable vehicle for me.

Specificity is important. The more specific you are when you word your intention, the more likely you are to receive exactly what you desire, as long as it hurts no one and is for the highest good of all concerned. Consequently, you can make the intention for the new car even more specific by phrasing it thusly:

> I wish to obtain a brand new 328i BMW red convertible within the

THE POWER OF MAGIC FOR MANIFESTATION

next 2 months that I easily afford and is a dependable and enjoyable vehicle for me.

You can now see how very specific you can be when you word your intention. I could go on to say I wish for the 328i to have a tan leather interior, a stereo system with Bose speakers, and so on.

You may have to write your intention several times before you arrive at one that is specific enough and to your liking. Now it's time to direct your focus into your intention, which you do by stating the intention seven times either aloud or to yourself in your head.

The next step is directing your thought toward manifesting your desire. As you grow more proficient with spell-casting, you perform this step simultaneously while placing your focus into the intention. For beginners, I have separated these as two mutually exclusive steps in the process, but, as you will see, the more you practice, they are really a single step.

In order to direct your thought, as you read your intention see your intention becoming real. Feel it. Imagine what it would be like to sit behind the wheel of that 328i. Imagine people's heads turning as you drive down the boulevard in your red convertible with the top down and your hair blowing in the wind. Imagine what that would feel like physically as well as emotionally.

Maintain your directed thought by visualizing your desired intention already manifested into reality as though it has already occurred. See yourself owning that 328i BMW. See yourself driving it and enjoying the experience.

There is no set time required for holding a directed thought. I will tell you that beginners who have never meditated or practiced any form of magic may find it difficult at first to hold their focus and a directed thought for more than 20 seconds without another thought popping into their mind. For instance, let's say you mind is focusing on the car of your dreams. You see yourself driving that car. So far, so good. Then, let's say your stomach growls. You suddenly realize you're hungry and instead of remaining focused on your dream car, you start to think of a nice, big juicy burger. Your focus and thought process is now broken, so what to do?

Merely bring your attention back to your original intention and resume your focus and directed thought. Try to hold it for 30 seconds, then with practice extend that to one minute, then eventually up to two minutes. Personally, I have never maintained my focus and directed thought on a desired outcome for longer than two minutes and I have always been very successful in my spell work.

You may ask, but what about the use of candles and anointing them with oils; and the use of herbs I have heard or read so much about? Doesn't that matter? The answer to that question is yes and no.

I refer to herbs, candles, oils and anything else used as magical accoutrements. They are like fashion accessories. It's nice to have the latest Coach purse or Jimmy Choo shoes; however, it's not necessary to life as we know it (some may argue that point, though). The same applies to the use of magical accoutrements. They are not 100% necessary for your spell work to be effective. In fact, they are not necessary at all. Scott Cunningham (1989:25) states that such tools are not necessary, but they can "enrich rituals and symbolize complex energies. The tools have no power save for that which we lend to them."

In other words, if it adds to your comfort level to use candles, herbs, oils, crystals, incense, a wand, and other magical tools when you perform spells, then by all means do so. As a Wicca instructor, I never encourage any of my students to do anything with which they feel uncomfortable. That uncomfortable "this-isn't-quite-right-for-me" feeling leads to failure every single time. When you are at ease and feeling confident about what you are doing you are much more likely to meet with success. This not only applies to magic, but to all areas of life.

I consider it beyond the scope of this book to discuss the use of tools in magic, but if you are searching for more information, I refer you to the works of Scott Cunningham and Silver RavenWolf that are listed in the Resources at the end of this book.

MAGICAL ASSOCIATIONS OF THE CARDS

Based upon their interpretations and/or imagery, each card is associated with certain magical intentions. Feel free to also use your own best judgment and intuition when choosing which cards to use for your spell work. For example, just because I recommend here that the Rider card can be used to represent your wish for a new car, this does not mean you need to use that particular card. The Key card may represent a car to you more than the Rider card does, so by all means use whichever cards you are the most comfortable with and can focus upon the easiest. On the following page is a list of magical associations for each card.

THE POWER OF MAGIC FOR MANIFESTATION

1. RIDER

Car, mail service, short trip by car. The Rider card can be used to help manifest a new car, help to find a good mechanic to repair a car, or to sell a car. Other vehicles can also be indicated, such as a motorcycle or bicycle.

2. CLOVER

Good luck, gambling, the lotto. The Clover can be used to help manifest good luck, or an improvement in your luck. The Clover also means something can occur within a short time, so if you wish for something to happen within a short time frame, use The Clover.

3. SHIP

Sailing, water sports, travel over water (either by ship or by plane), international commerce and trade. The Ship can be used when planning a trip to help all things run smoothly. The Ship can also represent a journey of consciousness as well, so this card can also be used in matters pertaining to astral traveling or dreams.

4. HOUSE

Anything to do with the home and/or family. In order to sell a house, I recommend using House + Sacred Cow. In order to purchase a house or move to a new one, try Ibis + House. The House card is used when you need to focus energy on your physical home—whether that is an actual house, apartment, or a single room you rent from someone, it does not matter. The House card represents your home. The House card can be used when repairs need to be made, to help create a more peaceful environment should there be any discord, or if you are hoping to buy a home or move from one home to another. The House card also represents the family, so it can be used for magic pertaining to the family, but this should be family members who are all under the same roof.

5. TREE

Health, the family, stability, grounding your energy.

6. CLOUDS

Technically, this is seen as a negative card, so I do not recommend its use, since it would represent confusion, mental issues, and misunderstandings. You may wish to use it to represent recent misunderstands, then follow it with the Sun card to represent those misunderstandings clearing up.

7. SNAKE

As with Clouds, when examined from a magical standpoint, Snake is also negative. I would recommend using it in order to cleanse a person or location from negativity. The Snake card would represent the actual negative energy in need of cleansing, and you could then follow it with a card that represents the act of cleansing, such as Water Lily or Sun for a clearing up and general healing.

8. SARCOPHAGUS

Endings, communication with the dead. Spirit communication is something I do not recommend if you are brand new to such things. However, this card can be used to represent your spirit guides, if you are interested in contacting them. If so, then follow this card with the Birds, which represents communication, and conclude with the Stars or Key card to denote success.

9. FLOWERS

Joy, happiness, gifts, healing.

10. SICKLE

Used to represent cuts, harm, or illness. Since it's also a negative card, precede it with a positive card to help bring healing, such as Tree, Sun, Flowers, or Water Lily. Remember, the direction in which the blade faces, which here is to the right, will cut into the card to the right, thus diminishing or harming it in some way. Use a positive card to precede Sickle and that card combination will represent harvesting whatever is represented by the preceding card.

11. CROOK & FLAIL

Authority, parents, teachers, the law. If you are using Crook & Flail to represent a parent or set of parents or a teacher, follow it with the God and Goddess cards, or the Pharaoh and Priestess cards. If you are using the card to represent authority such as the law, follow it with Obelisk, then with a third card to represent what you wish to manifest. For example, for a positive judgment in court you may wish to use the card combination: Crook & Flail + Obelisk + Flowers.

12. BIRDS

Communication. The Birds card can be used in enchantments having to do with any type of verbal communication (the Letter is used for written communication, see below). The Birds can also be used to represent gossip or an older couple.

THE POWER OF MAGIC FOR MANIFESTATION

13. CHILD

Children, new projects. Use the Child card to represent an actual child, or if you wish for a fresh start in a situation, or to represent something small in size.

14. DESERT FOX

Work (if this is your Work card), deceit, treachery. Desert Fox is a negative card when used in a magical manner so you would use Desert Fox to represent a person who is lying or behaving in a treacherous manner. If protection is required, you may wish to follow this card with Sacred Cow, Dog, or Key.

15. SACRED COW

Mother, motherhood, mother-in-law, finances, strength, protection. If you are using Sacred Cow to represent a woman, I would recommend pairing it with the Goddess or Priestess card to create a firmer connection with the mother figure.

16. STARS

Success, esoteric studies. Stars is a good card to use if you wish to perform a spell to increase your own intuitive abilities.

17. IBIS

Changes in general, relocation of home in particular. The combination of Ibis + House can be used in a spell to find a new home.

18. DOG

Friend, loyalty, and faithfulness, a pet dog, guidance, protection.

19. OBELISK

Authority, corporations, big business, hospitals, schools, jails and other types of large institutions.

20. GARDEN

Socializing, parties, concerts (attending or actual performance).

THE POWER OF MAGIC FOR MANIFESTATION

21. MOUNTAIN

Yet another card with negative connotations, Mountain represents blocks, obstacles, delays, and enemies. You may wish to use this card to represent one or more of these undesired things and combine it with another card to banish such energies from your life. I would therefore recommend that you have Mountain follow the card whose energies you wish to decrease in your life, such as Mice + Mountain would represent the decrease of anxiety or limiting the chance of something being stolen.

22. CROSSROADS

Choices, the need to come to a decision.

23. MICE

A negative card denoting fears, worries, loss, or theft, you may wish to decrease or banish such things from your life. Therefore, you may wish to use the card combination of Mice + Mountain, or Mice + Djed Pillar. Mountain blocks things while Djed Pillar can bring things to a standstill.

24. HEART

Love, romance, romantic relationships.

25. RING

Commitments of all kinds, including business partnerships. If you desire marriage, use the combination of Ring + Heart to represent a further commitment in a romantic relationship.

26. SCROLL

Education and secrets. You can use Obelisk + Scroll to represent a school or university, for example. If someone has been keeping secrets from you the you can use the combination of Scroll + Mountain to attempt to stop this type of behavior.

27. LETTER

Documents, diplomas, prescriptions, anything of a written nature.

28. GOD AND PHARAOH

A man.

THE POWER OF MAGIC FOR MANIFESTATION

29. GODDESS AND PRIESTESS

A woman.

30. WATER LILY

Peace, harmony, purity, wisdom, old age.

31. SUN

Success, healing, achievement.

32. MOON

Work (if the Moon is your Work card), honors, recognition, creativity. When used in combination with other cards, the first card should represent that area for which you wish to receive honors or recognition, then follow that card with the Moon. For example, if you wish for honors for a thesis you are writing, use the combination of Scroll + Moon.

33. KEY

Success, opportunities, the opening of doors, clearing the way ahead. The Key card is excellent for removing obstacles from your path. Use it as the second card in the combination of Mountain + Key to denote successful removal or elimination of obstacles or delays.

34. FISH

Money, abundance. The combination of Fish + Clover would represent money gained via gambling or the lotto, for example. Your Work card followed by Fish would represent money gained through your own work.

35. ANCHOR

Stability, safety. If your wish is for a stable marriage, use the card combination of Ring + Anchor. If you wish for a stable job, use the combination of your Work card + Anchor. Stability in the home environment would be House + Anchor.

THE POWER OF MAGIC FOR MANIFESTATION

36. DJED PILLAR

Suffering, pain, guilt, grief. Arguably the most negative card in the Lenormand system, Djed Pillar ideally should never be used for magical purposes unless you are striving to decrease something negative in your life. For example, if you have recently lost a loved one and are suffering from excessive grief you may wish to consider using the card combination of Djed Pillar + Mountain. This combination can help to put a stop to the grief, and followed by Flowers can bring in energy to help you regain your sense of happiness. However, I do not recommend use of the Djed Pillar for magical intentions.

37. CAT

Attention to details, alertness, sharpening your senses, agility.

EGYPTIAN DEITIES ASSOCIATED WITH THE CARDS

Each card within *The Egyptian Lenormand* is associated with one or more particular gods or goddesses. You may wish to keep this in mind when performing spells with the cards, as certain cards can be used to represent particular deities upon whom you may wish to call upon for extra help in manifesting your desires. These associations are based either on the particular deity who channeled the card to me or associations the ancient Egyptians would have had based upon what is depicted on the card and the associations of those items and/or places with particular deities.

CARD TITLE	DEITY
1. RIDER	Osiris, Ra
2. CLOVER	Khumn
3. SHIP	Anubis, Isis
4. HOUSE	Isis, Hathor, Bastet
5. TREE	Isis, Sekhmet, Osiris
6. CLOUDS	Tefnut, goddess of moisture and rain
7. SNAKE	Apep
8. SARCOPHAGUS	Osiris
9. FLOWERS	Isis, Hathor, and Bastet
10. SICKLE	Set
11. CROOK & FLAIL	Osiris, Horus, Amun-Ra
12. BIRDS	Horus
13. CHILD	Horus

THE POWER OF MAGIC FOR MANIFESTATION

14. DESERT FOX	Set	26. SCROLL	Thoth
15. SACRED COW	Hathor, Nut	27. LETTER	Thoth
16. STARS	Nut	28. GOD AND PHAROAH	Amun-Ra
17. IBIS	Thoth	29. GODDESS AND PRIESTESS	Isis
18. DOG	Anubis (Greek name); Anpu (ancient Egyptian name)	30. WATER LILY	Isis, Hathor, Bastet
19. OBELISK	Amun	31. SUN	Khepera and Ra
20. GARDEN	Isis, Hathor, and Bastet	32. MOON	Thoth
21. MOUNTAIN	Geb	33. KEY	Amun-Ra
22. CROSSROADS	Set	34. FISH	Osiris
23. MICE	Set and Sekhmet	35. ANCHOR	Anubis
24. HEART	Isis, Osiris, Hathor, Bastet	36. DJED PILLAR	Osiris
25. RING	Isis and Osiris	37. CAT	Bastet

A SAMPLE SPELL

I will now provide an example of how you can put all this information to work for you. Many people come to me to perform candle work for them and the most popular type of candle work I perform pertains to matters of the heart. Hypothetically, let's say there is a client—I'll call her Christy. Christy has had a number of relationships in the past that have failed. There is a guy at work to whom she is attracted, but she's not sure he has any interest in her. She comes asking if I will perform a spell to get the two of them together so they can start dating.

First, I inform her we cannot use magic to control another person's decision-making process. To do so would be manipulative, and therefore dark magic. Instead, I recommend she focus on attracting a person to her who is perfect for her and vice versa. It may be that man at work or someone completely different whom she may have not even met. Christy agrees.

Using the cards as my only magical tool, plus the ability to write an intention, to focus, and maintain a sustained thought about the intention, I get to work. For a new love with the intention that this person be a perfect fit—perhaps even a soul mate—I would word the intention for Christy as follows:

I [meaning Christy] wish for a new man in my life who is kind, loving, supportive of my endeavors, desires children, will make an excellent father and husband, who has a good career and is a good provider, is healthy, and who has all the same interests as I do. I ask for this or something better.

Remember to always conclude your intention with what I call the "magical caveat," "I ask for this or something better."

I would then give this intention to Christy and ask her to focus upon it off and on for a few days until I perform her spell. On the day I perform her spell, I would then tell her to concentrate on her intention throughout the day and evening whenever she gets an opportunity. This is how she can lend her own personal energy to the proceedings.

Next, I choose the cards to represent Christy's intention. Considering this spell is about new love, I definitely would need to use the Heart card. Since she is also interested in a life-long commitment, Ring is also necessary. I would also add Flowers for happiness, Child to represent desired children, and I would round it out by including Tree for health and Fish for prosperity. The card spread on my altar for Christy would therefore look like this:

Heart + Ring + Flowers + Child + Tree + Fish.

There is no set limit as to how many cards you can use. The only requirement is that each card must match a part of the intention.

THE POWER OF MAGIC FOR MANIFESTATION

At this point if you wish, you can add candles, herbs, oils, and incense or use any other magical tools, such as crystals. This is up to you.

Once you have your items in place on your altar, write longhand two copies of the intention. Since I am working on Christy's behalf, I would also write her full name, date of birth, and current location on a slip of paper. You do that only once when working for someone else. If you are working only for yourself no additional slip of paper is needed, since you are there in person to add your energy to the proceedings.

I would then place the slip of paper on the first, or subject card, of the spread for the spell. The first card of any spell's spread should represent the main focus of the intention, in this case, a new romantic relationship. Next, I would place one copy of the intention on top of the slip of paper with Christy's information that I have already placed on top of the Heart card.

I then concentrate on her intention, repeating it seven times to myself (you can do this silently or aloud, it doesn't matter and one is not more powerful than the other). I picture Christy as being happy with a man and having all the things she desires in a romantic relationship.

Once I have held that image for two minutes (when you start out this may be difficult, so 20-30 seconds is enough for beginners), I then bend over and breathe the intention (while still focusing directed thought on seeing Christy happy with a man) into the spread of cards on my altar. Breathing out with my mouth from left to right along the line of cards shares part of my life force with the cards in order to help bring Christy's intention to life.

At this point, the actual performance of the spell is complete. I would then allow the cards to remain on my altar, overnight if possible, then the next day I would pick up the slips of paper and re-shuffle the cards used back into the full deck. Then, if you are working for yourself, you can glue or tape one copy of the intention into a journal and also include the date and the cards you used for your spell. This is an excellent manner with which you can keep track of your spell work and see which card combinations are fruitful for you and which are not. The second copy of the intention needs to be given to Nature. You should fold it and bury it somewhere on your property. If you are renting, burying the intention in a potted plant works just as well.

The next and final step is to release the intention by simply letting it go. Do not dwell on it, wondering if your spell will work and how long it will take. Instead, have faith it will all work out as it is meant to: in divine time and in divine order.

SUMMARY

Magic can be performed for any purpose you can imagine. Major categories of magic spells are: prosperity, love, protection, healing, and banishing (sending away undesired energies or elements of our lives). Intentions should be worded as specifically as you can manage and, then, with the proper focus and directed thought, you will be more likely to manifest your desires into reality.

In summary, the magic you perform should always be of a positive nature. Life is too short and too full of strife to be focusing negative thoughts toward others. Always keep in mind that no matter how negative or harmful a situation may become, there is always a positive way to deal with it. Search your heart and discover for yourself how best to handle it; then work your magic with the highest good of yourself and all concerned always guiding every magical intention you ever create. That way, you cannot go wrong.

CONCLUSION

It is my hope that you enjoy using *The Egyptian Lenormand* and that you also make use of other Lenormand decks, of which there are now quite a few, especially of the self-published variety. Lenormand is gaining in popularity everyday as new people are discovering a 200+-year-old method of divination. The Lenormand system is simple, straight-forward, can be quite literal, and it gives clear answers with uncanny accuracy.

It is my wish that in some small way *The Egyptian Lenormand* contributes to the expansion of your spiritual horizons. May the gods always smile upon you and may the cards always hold only good things for you and your loved ones.

Wishing You All Many Blessings,

Nefer Khepri, PhD., R. M-T.
Houston, Texas

REFERENCES CITED

Alm, Brian. Ancient Egyptian Religion—Part 4: Preparing for Eternity. Egyptological. www.egyptological.com/2012/02/ancient-egyptian-religion-part-4-preparing-for-eternity-7307. 2012.

Amarak, Keith. Deck Activation Ceremony. Online Lenormand class assignment. 2013.

Athanasiou, Aristea. Deck Activation Ceremony. Online Lenormand class assignment. 2013.

Bauval, Robert and Adrian Gilbert. *The Orion Mystery: Unlocking the Secrets of the Pyramids*. Crown: New York. 1995.

Birjou, Salisha Noor. Deck Activation Ceremony. Online Lenormand class assignment. 2013

Boroshevengra, Andy. *Lenormand Thirty Six Cards: Fortune-Telling with the Petit Lenormand: Part One - The 36 Symbols and their Meanings & Appendix 4 - Health Combinations*. Kindle E-Book, self-published 2014

Brown, Vincent. 2002. The Concept of the Djed Symbol. Pyramid of Man. www.pyramidofman.com/Djed/. 2013.

Cortez, Ana and C.J. Freeman. 2002. *The Playing Card Oracles: A Source Book for Divination*. U.S. Games. 2007.

Cunningham, Scott. *Wicca: A Guide for the Solitary Practitioner*. Llewellyn Publications: St. Paul, MN. 1989.

DenElder. Personal Communication. Discussion of Interpretations of the Cat Card. 2013.

Duquette, Milo Lon. *The Book of Ordinary Oracles*. Red Wheel Weiser, LLC: Newburyport, MA. 2005.

Faulkner, Raymond O., trans. *Ancient Egyptian Book of the Dead*. Barnes and Noble Publishing. Original edition 1972, The Limited Edition Club, New York. 2005.

Galili, Ehud, Jacob Sharvit, Michal Artzy. "Reconsidering Byblian and Egyptian Stone Anchors Using Numeral Methods: New Finds From the Israeli Coast." *The International Journal of Nautical Archaeology,* Vol. 23.2:93-107. Portsmouth, UK .1994.

George, Rana. Personal Communication, 4/9/2013. Lenormand Card Study Group, Facebook.com.

Georgiou, Marijana. Deck Activation Ceremony. Online Lenormand class assignment. 2013.

Globerover. Egyptian Lotus Flower. Country Facts: The World at Your Fingertips. http://www.kwintessential.co.uk/articles/egypt/Egyptian-Lotus-Flower/3246. 2010.

Greer, Mary K. Personal Communication. Lenormand Card Study Group, Facebook.com. 2013.

REFERENCES CITED

Hancock, Graham and Robert Bauval. *The Message of the Sphinx: A Quest for the Hidden Legacy of Mankind.* Crown. New York. 1996.

Hetchel, Johann Kaspar. *Das Speil der Hoffnung* (*The Game of Hope*). Gustav Phillip Jakob Bieling, publisher. 1798.

Imhotep, Asar. Posture and Meaning: Interpreting Egyptian Art Through a Kongo Cultural Lens. http://www.asarimhotep.com/index.php/articles/18-posture-and-meaning-interpreting-egyptian-art-through-a-kongo-cultural-lens. 2012.

Krause, Bernadette Hyde. Deck Activation Ceremony. Online Lenormand class assignment. 2013.

Krontz, Susan Keen. Deck Activation Ceremony. Online Lenormand class assignment. 2013.

Myasliwiec, Karol. *The Twilight of Ancient Egypt: First Millenium B. C. E.* Cornell University Press: Ithaca, NY. 2000.

Nance, Evie.. Deck Activation Ceremony. Online Lenormand class assignment. 2013.

Olson, Jessica. Personal Communication. Lenormand Cards and Locations. Online Lenormand class. 2013.

Olson, Jessica. Deck Activation Ceremony. Online Lenormand class assignment. 2013.

Oushy, Hamdy. Fact Sheet: Egyptian Clover. Afghanistan Water, Agriculture, and Technology Transfer (AWATT) Program. New Mexico State University: Las Cruces, NM. 2008.

Parsons, Marie. The Valley of the Kings. Tour Egypt. www.touregypt.net/featurestories/valley.htm. 1996-2012.

Parsons, Marie. Egypt: Women in Religion in the Old Kingdom, Part 1. Tour Egypt. http://www.touregypt.net/featurestories/women1.htm. 2011.

Pitt, Kyle. Hieroglyphics and the Egyptians 4,000 B. C. Kyle Pitt's Portfolio. http://pittkyle123.wordpress.com/2011/03/10/hieroglyphics-and-the-egyptians-4000-bc/. 2011.

Plutarch. Plutarch's De Iside Et Osiride. English translation and notes by J. Gwyn Griffiths. University of Wales Press: South Glamorgan, UK. 1970.

Riding, Helen. Le Petit Lenormand Eclectique: A text companion. Edmund Zewbrowski, et. al. The La Petit Lenormand Eclectique Facebook group. Facebook.com. 2013.

Riding, Helen. Personal Communication. Lenormand Card Study Group, Facebook.com. 2013.

Rose, Sama. Deck Activation Ceremony. Online Lenormand class assignment. 2013.

Seid, Timothy W., PhD. Interpreting Ancient Manuscripts Web. Earlham School of Religion. http://legacy.earlham.edu/~seidti/iam/papyrus.html. 2004.

RESOURCES

Burack, Marsha Jean. *Reiki: Healing Yourself and Others. A Photo-Instructional Art Book*. Lo Ro Productions. Reiki Healing Institute. Encinitas, California. 1995.

Clark, Rosemary. *The Sacred Tradition in Ancient Egypt*. Llewellyn Publications: St. Paul, MN. 2000.

Clark, Rosemary. *The Sacred Magic of Ancient Egypt*. Llewellyn Publications: St. Paul, MN. 2003.

Cunningham, Scott. *Wicca: A Guide for the Solitary Practitioner*. Llewellyn Publications: St. Paul, MN. 1998.

Lurker, Manfred. *An Illustrated Dictionary of The Gods and Symbols of Ancient Egypt*. Barbara Cummings, trans. Thames and Hudson: NY, New York. 1996.

Matthews, Caitlin. *The Complete Lenormand Oracle Handbook: Reading the Language and Symbols of the Cards*. Destiny Books. Rochester, Vermont. 2014.

Mercatante, Anthony S. *Who's Who in Egyptian Mythology*. Clarkson N. Potter, Inc. Publishers: New York, NY. 1978.

RavenWolf, Silver. *To Ride a Silver Broomstick*. Llewellyn Publications: St. Paul, MN. 1993.

RavenWolf, Silver. *To Stir a Magic Cauldron*. Llewellyn Publications: St. Paul, MN. 1996.

RavenWolf, Silver. 1999. *To Light a Sacred Flame*. Llewellyn Publications: St. Paul, MN. 1999.

Schoch, Robert M. *Voices in the Rocks: A Scientist Looks at Catastrophes and Ancient Civilizations*. Harmony Publishing: New York. 1999.

Watterson, Barbara. *Gods of Ancient Egypt*. Bramley Books Limited: Surrey, England, UK. 1999.

Stead, Miriam. *Egyptian Life*. British Museum, London. 1986.

Steinbach, Sylvie. *The Secrets of the Lenormand Oracle*. Self-published, CreateSpace.com. Lexington, KY. 2007.

Suttie, J. M. Trifolium alexandrinum L. www.fao.org/ag/AGP/AGPC/doc/Gbase/DATA/PF000414.HTM. 1999.

Treppner, Iris. *The Parlour of Sybyll* (Die Sibylle der Salons Bianca Heers, trans. Kindle E-Book Edition. 2013.

Watterson, Barbara. *Gods of Ancient Egypt*. Bramley Books. Ltd.: Surrey, United Kingdom. 1999.

Wegner, Jennifer Houser. Something's Fishy in the Palace of Merneptah: Graffiti in Ancient Egypt. Beyond the Gallery Walls. Penn Museum Blog. penn.museum/blog/museum/somethings-fishy-in-the-palace-of-merneptah-graffiti-in-ancient-egypt/. 2011.